It's not about what makes us happy, it is about *how we create happiness!* Discover how your SMILE can create a new life for you!

Here is what people are saying about *The Smile Prescription*...

"It is my life's calling to create value by connecting the most successful, brightest, and amazing leaders in this world. Before I learned about *The Smile Prescription*, I never realized how much this hinged on my ability to make people smile. I am privileged to know Dr. Rich as a business associate and dear friend, and you must see what he is doing. Relationships will grow when they have a lot of smiles. Relationships without smiles will die. Create more smiles in your life and your relationships NOW with *The Smile Prescription*."

Larry Benet, The Connector,
Forbes 25 Professional Networking Experts to Watch in 2015

"Dr. Rich masterfully uses the latest scientific research to reveal what makes business and personal relationships thrive or fail. His unique expertise as an accomplished facial surgeon brings a fresh perspective to the age-old question: How do you really create and measure happiness? *The Smile Prescription* explores the art of smiling, facial expression, and innovative communication strategies that will absolutely make a difference in your life and bottom line. Dr. Rich is the original "Smile Dr." and I recommend *The Smile Prescription* to anyone who wants to grow professionally or personally."

Scott Hallman, Two–Time Inc. 500 Founder & CEO and
World's Leading Business Coach

"Working as an actor and top level coach in Hollywood, the foundation of what I teach is facial expression. Everyone should read *The Smile Prescription* because nothing is more effective in conveying trust, rapport, and emotional impact than how we use our smile. Dr. Rich's approach with *The Smile Prescription* is a fantastic look at the simplest and purest form of how people connect with one another. When I read this powerful book, I started smiling and haven't stopped since! Share your smile now. If the eyes are the window to the soul then the smile is the shining light."

Thom McFadden, Hollywood's Coach to the Stars

"Dr. Rich will change your thinking about how and why we smile. His insight is brilliant and his thought experiments are elegant. He sees the topic only as a physician and scientist could. Who knew you can measure the intelligence of a smile? You will absolutely learn valuable strategies to use at home and in the office, and you need to share this with those you care about most. I have seen results with my team, my patients, and most importantly with my family. My sincere thanks to Dr. Rich for helping me to create more happiness in my life and in my business. There is no doubt in my mind that you will love this book!"

Dr. Frank Bono, Cofounder of Gulfcoast Spine Institute and the BioSpine Institute

"Traditional wisdom focuses too much on mind over body. *The Smile Prescription* takes a scientific, but playful and personal, counterpoint to explore body over the mind through the power of smile. Throughout the pages of *The Smile Prescription* Dr. Rich makes it easy to see how smiles transform yourself and those around you. *The Smile Prescription* inspires readers to understand the messages and emotions generated through smiling, as well as how to incorporate this act into your daily routine. I'm confident that by embracing Dr. Rich's insight and your own smile, you will see benefits in your personal and professional relationships immediately."

Jonathan Gorab, Director at PwC

"For physicians and health-care administrators, it is more important than ever that we use the power of smiling to care for our patients, communicate with our teams, and guide doctors through the challenges that lay ahead. Today's leaders in public health, both nationally and internationally, all understand how smiling impacts our patients and our teams. Redesigning America's health care system we invoke the proverb 'Physician, heal thyself,' and one of the best healing medicines we have is our smile."

David Massaro, MD, Deputy Chief Medical Officer, VA MidSouth Healthcare Network

"With clients and business contacts across the country and internationally, it is critical that I do everything I can to build strong relationships. These invaluable lessons in *The Smile Prescription* are based in scientific research, proven medical wisdom, and the latest strategies for high performance. Dr. Rich translates complex medical knowledge so that it is teachable and applicable to anyone at any level. These key concepts and communication skills foster team-building, customer service, and personal development. Now everyone has access to these simple and effective tools that absolutely work. Dr. Rich is masterfully introducing a new era in personal health and happiness with a smile movement that will certainly make an impact in our world. You can not afford to miss what *The Smile Prescription* is teaching!"

Emile Allen, MD, Behavioral Modification Expert

"I've known Dr. Rich his entire medical career, so I was not surprised to discover he was writing this book because he practices what he preaches. *The Smile Prescription* teaches you the positive outlook on life he has shared with me and many others over the years. In the financial services industry in which I work, our business is built on forming meaningful relationships with other people. What better way to engage with another human being than to be present with them and offer them a smile? If you too work in a client service industry, you need to read this book and challenge yourself with *The Smile Prescription*!"

Andrew Grinstead, CEO of Leavell Investment Management

"In a world starved for positive emotions, it is remarkable to see how we can move ourselves by remembering to smile, whether it's when we are alone, or with others. *The Smile Prescription* is needed in today's world, when the tides of sadness and despair can seem almost overwhelming. It is a powerful reminder that we can always do something. Perhaps none of us individually can or will change the world, but we can change OUR world, and that is what smiling will do for each of us."

Al Davis, Belmont MA

"This isn't just a book to read, it's a "Smile Prescription" to take and master. I can assure you that if you apply what you learn, the value is priceless."

Dr. Rich

The Smile Prescription

Printed in the United States

10 9 8 7 6 5 4 3 2 1

For More Information, please visit ImageLift.com

DISCLAIMER - The content of this book is for informational purposes only and does not constitute a patient physician relationship. Any medical questions should be directed towards your doctor. If you or someone you know are in need of assistance now for depression or suicidal thoughts, please call 1-800-273-8255 (1-800-273-TALK) or visit www.suicidepreventionlifeline. org Names used for patient stories have been changed and stories have been edited to protect the anonymity of the patients."

Published in New York, New York, by Morgan James Publishing. Morgan James and The Entrepreneurial Publisher are trademarks of Morgan James, LLC. www. MorganJamesPublishing.com.

The Morgan James Speakers Group can bring authors to your live event. For more information or to book an event visit The Morgan James Speakers Group at www. TheMorganJamesSpeakersGroup.com.

A free eBook edition is available with the purchase of this print book.

CLEARLY PRINT YOUR NAME ABOVE IN UPPER CASE

Instructions to claim your free eBook edition:
1. Download the Shelfie app for Android or iOS
2. Write your name in **UPPER CASE** above
3. Use the Shelfie app to submit a photo
4. Download your eBook to any device

ISBN 9781630478247 (paperback)

ISBN 9781630478254 (eBook)

ISBN 9781630476151 (hardcover)

Library of Congress Control Number: 2015918165

Cover and Interior Design by:

Bob Bubnis

booksetters121@aol.com

In an effort to support local communities, raise awareness and funds, Morgan James Publishing donates a percentage of all book sales for the life of each book to Habitat for Humanity Peninsula and Greater Williamsburg.

Get involved today, visit www.MorganJamesBuilds.com.

THE
SMILE
PRESCRIPTION

RICH CASTELLANO, MD
THE SMILE DR.

NEW YORK

To Irene and my family -
the smiles that make me
who I am.

Thank you to Thom McFadden, Bruce Barbour, and Bob Bubnis for your commitment and dedication to change lives through this message.

TABLE OF C☺NTENTS:

"I am smiling. Didn't you get my :) emoticon?"

chapter one

"FACING" LIFE

Life Can Kill Your Smile, and Smiling Can Save Your Life

"Beauty is that which makes us smile. We may experience something that is beautiful to our senses, or we may give a beautiful meaning to a person, event, or object. The more beauty we see, feel, hear, and touch, the more we are inspired to smile." — Dr. Rich

"To be yourself in a world that is constantly trying to make you something else is the greatest accomplishment." — Ralph Waldo Emerson

Humble Beginnings

It all started when I was seven years old. Life was free, fun, full of play, and limitless. I had what I thought was a happy home and loving parents, and I had no idea what was coming when I developed a deep, painful ache in my left hip. Unfortunately, this went on to become a chronic and life-changing bone condition that forced me to spend two-and-a-half years in a wheelchair and on crutches. The doctors agreed that I would have a limp for the rest of my life. I was numb and horrified. I was told I would be put in an "A-frame" leg brace and would have to walk around like a stick figure. I have always been thankful that Mom never allowed that brace.

As I did my best to recover, there were a lot of tears. I needed to be accepted and acknowledged by the other kids. It was painful to be bullied and called names. I felt excluded and invisible, and compared to those around me it seemed my body was crippled and not natural. During this time, Mom was struggling with schizophrenia, and my parents got a divorce which took years to settle. During the separation, Mom took my brothers and I to live with my family out-of-state. It seemed as if my whole world and family had turned upside-down, and as a child I felt completely out of control and depressed.

2 ½ years in a wheelchair and on crutches changed me forever.

Yet I was able to move on from this...And with the help of my family, I kept smiling!

I still had family that cared for me, and the doctors I saw were kind and compassionate. Despite these challenges, I had a lot to be thankful for. When I look back, this was one of my big "aha moments," when I first realized I would become a physician and have the same impact on the lives of others. While I was healing my hip, I was confused and scared, and my deepest fear was that my condition was untreatable. With the help of my family and faith, I put on my best smile and I started my road to recovery. My doctors would joke with me to make me smile, and it made me feel better. I made it through and I learned to walk normally again (and even became the captain of my high school tennis team). I learned a very important lesson: No matter how bad it got, there was always something to smile about. Smiling was the cure that changed my whole life. :) I learned this from my Dad who smiled no matter what happened to him. He loved making people smile, and as a dentist he worked on people's smiles all day long. He always made me laugh and smile and I loved him very much. He was my hero.

We all go through challenges in life that push us to our limits. When we are forced to dig a little deeper, we realize we always have more to smile about. I used this lesson to get me through many stages of my life. Helping my mom with her mental illness was exasperating. She tried to convince me that my father was a part of the mafia and had murdered people. What is worse, she said he was trying to kill her too. Her life was surrounded with fear and paranoia. There was no laughter or smiling in her pain.

It was a huge burden for my family. No one understood her, and we were embarrassed to admit there was a problem. I did my best to make her happy and smile, and we just looked harder for things to be grateful for and reasons to smile. I was shocked to learn that as many as 1 in 200 people[1] are diagnosed with schizophrenia. In the face of these challenges, I still found the strength to excel in college and get accepted to medical school. When times got tough for the unbelievable amount of work required for medical training and residency, I just had faith that God had bigger plans for my life and did my best to keep smiling. And boy, did he ever!

Overcoming my hip disease would have never happened without the power of a smile.

When I was going through my surgical training, I met and married the woman of my dreams, Irene. She definitely put a smile on my face and we made a great team together! Now I had someone to smile with, and I no longer felt alone. What a great feeling! :) We now have three beautiful children and an amazing family that we dearly love. With her assistance, I became a successful double board certified facial plastic surgeon with patients from all around the world, which of course carries even bigger challenges yet. I love caring for my patients like they are my family. What a gift it is to be invited into someone's deepest vulnerabilities, and then to take this privilege and help them smile and change their life for the better. Nothing compares to the emotional feeling it gives me when my patients smile.

It reminds me of the Japanese Proverb, "Fall seven times, stand up eight."

As I think back to medical school, I was influenced greatly by the detailed works of Rubens, Leonardo da Vinci, and many of the classical artists. The realism of the facial expression they captured was so moving I was awestruck. Body-image, facial expression, and self-image have always fascinated me. After all, what is more important to our identity than our face? I found I have something very special to share that has changed my life and helped me to cultivate a love of people. I'm dedicated to sharing this so that it will change your life too. Smiling has saved my health, my marriage, my business, and my life!

The happiness in my family comes from our smiles (:

I applaud the scientific community for proving the abilities of our smile as an untapped power. There are very specific strategies on how our facial muscles and behaviors can change our appearance to make us likeable, weak, strong, or unlikeable. Isn't it exciting that smiling has been proven to reduce pain and improve your recovery from stress? When I learned this, I was ecstatic because I knew I was on the right path to assist people to rediscover the joy and beauty within their lives.

I know you might be thinking, "What gives Dr. Rich the ability to make these distinctions?" Well here it is. As a double board certified facial plastic surgeon, and WSJ bestselling author, I am an expert on how to change our facial appearance AND on how our facial appearance changes us! My mission in life is to share this knowledge and help you use these simple yet powerful strategies to build your confidence and self-image to a new level. I absolutely guarantee it will make you *smile*, feel good about yourself, and IMPROVE YOUR SELF-ESTEEM!

Our world today has experienced a massive shift in cultural consciousness that has people seeking innovative solutions into health sustainability, social responsibility, and personal development. We now have the ability to live longer, grow stronger, and increase our quality of life. I'm excited to be a part of that! I love showing people the way to make a greater impact in their lives and in their relationships. It is wonderful that no matter how good our quality of life gets, we are always finding a way to make it even better yet. In today's world of instant information and rapidly advancing technology, *The Smile Prescription* is your personal GPS to guide you to better ways to connect and communicate. That puts a smile on my face. :) You have to think bigger than what you have seen before. *The Smile Prescription* allows you to make a change in your life and in your relationships right now.

When I first saw my daughter's face, she made me smile like I never have before. When she first opened her eyes, I did everything I could to show her my smile. Research has shown that smiling and laughter stimulate the reward centers in our brain.[2] Smiling is the gateway to laughter, one of the most powerful feelings in our body. Studies have demonstrated that laughter can protect the heart, burn calories, and even improve memory,[3-5] whether or not it makes milk come out of your nose. Yet, if everyone loves laughter so much, why do people smile so little?

As a facial plastic surgeon, it is easy for me to say a smile is Mother Nature's facelift! It is free and beautiful, it makes you look younger, and it makes you feel better! It is the facelift we should all do many times every day! In fact, I will ask you to smile RIGHT NOW. What are you waiting for? Feels good, right? If more people did this, there would be a lot fewer visits to plastic surgeons. There are no treatments performed in a plastic surgery office that compare to the beauty and power of a genuine smile.

Twenty smiles a day keeps the plastic surgeon away.—Dr. Rich

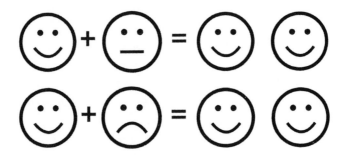

When we smile at others, it brings the smile out in their face, regardless of what they are doing.

The Power of Facial Expression With Ordinary Observations

Here's a fun exercise that you can play with: observe people like you are a detective. When you are walking around other people, put a smile on your face. It feels pretty good to share a smile with a stranger. Now, try it again, but this time do it without a smile and see what happens. Most people won't even look at you. There is very little interaction. How does that make you feel? If you are like me, it makes you feel empty or sad. Did you notice any difference? With rare exception, people treat you differently based on your facial expressions.

20

Have you noticed one of the first things people do when they see a baby? They smile! We want to baby-talk with them, coo, and make faces and smile. And what makes us smile bigger or even laugh? When the baby smiles back! The most powerful person in the world melts into a softie when a baby smiles at them.

It makes us feel good to see babies smile!

And what about our pets? Do they make us smile? Pets smile all the time, and it makes us feel great! When you get home and your dog is waiting to greet you, aren't they excited to see you? They are wagging their tail madly and jumping up and down. They make us smile, and that is why pets are a part of the family. Did you know that numerous research studies and scientific articles from Harvard, and scientists from across the world have proven that your smile can lower your blood pressure, relieve stress, boost your mood, get more out of relationships, and release endorphins? Those five are free. Your smile is one of the healthiest exercises your body can perform!

What happens the instant you see a loved one or a friend you haven't seen in a while? You smile at each other, laugh and embrace! I saw one of my classmates from high school at a hockey game, and as soon as I saw them we smiled and hugged and took a selfie together. And what about the most famous, most talked about masterpiece in the world? If you visit the Louvre in Paris, one of the first paintings you go to see is the mysterious smile of the *Mona Lisa*. So let's look at our smile on another level.

Babies make us smile!   Pets make us smile!

The Smile Prescription may be one of the most important books you will read in your life…

I think so, and here is why… ☺

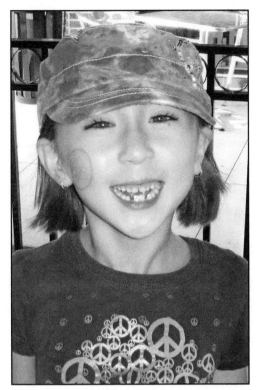

Why is *The Smile Prescription* so important?!?

I call this the "Fine Nine" benefits of *The Smile Prescription*:

1. Improving how others feel about you.

2. Looking more attractive.

3. Enhancing your creativity and likability!

4. Authenticity in your relationships.

5. Enjoying the now and being present.

6. Creating trust and rapport.

7. Building self-esteem and self-confidence.

8. Boosting health and busting stress.

9. Stimulating the pleasure centers with excitement and passion.

How can I make such bold statements as facts? It is because *The Smile Prescription* saved my marriage, my business, and my life. That is why it means so much to me to pass on this information. *The Smile Prescription* is like no other book written about smiling and happiness. I talk to people every day and I hear the same stories of frustration, sadness, and anger with their place in life. So many still do not have the results they are looking for. I would love for the whole world to smile and be happy! If you are like me, the idea of seeing everyone smile makes you want to laugh. Wouldn't that be great?

So let's just stop right now and reveal the magic of *The Smile Prescription*. As a kid I loved the birthday parties where a magician performed. I still remember trying to figure out how he did all of those amazing tricks. A good magician never tells their secrets, but get ready, because I am going to reveal the secret of *The Smile Prescription's* magic. Magic is an illusion that is impossible and real at the same time. Kind of sounds like life, doesn't it? Yet once you understand the illusion, it is no longer magic. But it is still magical to those that don't understand. When you can apply the illusion yourself, you become the magician. You can create magic anytime you need to! Check it out for yourself and see how magical it is.

Abracadabra...

You don't need a magic wand, but what you do need is to activate your creative imagination. It's a supposition, or as I like to call it, the magic "what if" game. What if you are cast as the star in a reality show called, "Your Happy Life"? That is a TV show worth watching! You start out in the morning, put a big smile on your face as you brush your teeth, because you're going to be making use of those pearly whites. :) You are getting ready to reveal to the world that you are the happiest person in town. Remember, it's a game, it's a role, and it needs to be fun. How would you walk? Would you jump for joy? Would you skip? Would you dance? Then do it, and have fun! Put some spring in your step! Don't censor yourself, this is the "what if" game, and you are creating magic for yourself and those around you. The healthiest of all human emotions come from smiling and laughing. That is the greatest medicine we have. The true magic of playing this game is how amazing smiling makes you (and those around you) feel! Nothing can compare to how good it feels to have a healthy smile and laugh. Pretty magical, don't you think? Just get started with your smile and you will see what I mean. :)

There is another name for this magical game: **The Smile Challenge!** What if you did this? What do you have to lose? Would you do it? Okay, then take the challenge!

The Smile Challenge is as simple as it sounds. Let's warm up by putting a smile on your face and see what happens! Felt good, didn't it? Do you think you can do this for fifteen minutes straight? You will be amazed at how it impacts your behavior towards those around you. It also changes how people respond to you. If you really want a big warm-up, try this for one hour! :)

Here is an easy and fun way to start the Smile Challenge: Share your smile with at least a dozen people and see if you can get them to smile. When you make eye contact, just saying "Hi" and smiling will usually work. Putting a solid smile on your face and saying "How are you?" will get a response 90 percent of the time. The eye contact is so important because you want to make sure that they see your smile. You will see by your success, that it is a natural reflex to return a smile. :)

The first time I experimented with the Smile Challenge, boy did I feel weird. I felt self-conscious, forced, and even a bit phony. But anytime you start a new habit, you will feel uncomfortable. That is the way we are. It's like brushing your teeth or writing your name with your non-dominant hand. It feels really funny at first because it isn't a part of your regular ritual. With time, it can feel natural and require no thought at all. It's like learning to tie your shoes. The more I smiled, the more I realized I was on the right track. I got goose bumps from the responses I received from everyone around me. I started looking forward to smiling because I knew what it would do. It made a real change inside of me and in those around me. My reluctance to smile in public changed into a habitual anticipation of engaging with people around me. Now I love to smile and I can't wait to get a response from people I meet. I must confess, I'm a smile addict!

Let me share with you how I got hooked. You know those days where nothing goes right? This was one of them. Nothing seemed to be going my way. I don't want to bore you with the details, but if anything bad could happen, it did. By the time I made it to my office, everything was behind. It felt like we were moving in slow motion while time was flying by. I pride myself on giving patients what they are looking for, but I had started out on the wrong foot. I was running from one patient to the next, and by trying to catch up, I did not have time to let my patients share everything they were feeling. What a bummer.

My next patient was sixty-three year old Sherry. She was a free spirit, and she loved riding her motorcycle. She is a big hugger, and would sometimes pinch my cheeks after hugging me and say, "You look TOO YOUNG to be doing this!" She had been waiting for over a year to do her facelift, it was a big decision for her. She had gone through a bad divorce, and for the first time in her life she felt free to be herself. Her confidence and self-esteem were at an all-time low, and she had made a decision to do something for herself. Today was her day of unveiling. I knew this was a very special day for her, and as I ran into the room, she gave me the evil eye as my staff were already unwrapping her bandages. "Thanks Dr. Rich, for finally showing up!"

I said, "I'm sorry, I got it Sherry, I'm here, I'm here…" This is the moment she had been looking forward to, and I was so focused on my artistry, the technical results, the healing, and the wound care that I forgot that it was her day and not mine. I was looking to see if she had broken stitches, or other post-surgical problems. My facial expression was as neutral and controlled as it could be considering how the day was going. My personality was flat, just like my pressed, sterile white coat: cool, and professional. She stared at me as I examined her face, and she gasped for air and yelled, "Oh No! I had a bad feeling about this!" as she covered her mouth with her hand as she started to cry. It looked like she was going to faint. I moved to her side and put my hand on her shoulders, "Sherry, Sherry, are you okay?" We put a blood pressure cuff on her arm and started measuring her oxygen level.

She wiped her eyes, looked up at me and said, "It's terrible, isn't it?"

I told her, "What do you mean, you look terrific!" I placed the mirror in front of her so she could see the results. It seemed like an eternity waiting for her response. Then she breathed a sigh of relief, and slowly a smile broke out on her face through the tears. I handed her a tissue and we all started smiling and laughing together.

"I was scared half to death when I saw the look on your face. I'm sorry, I'm such a big scaredy-cat, I just thought something had gone terribly wrong…" She said this as her smile grew bigger, and she started to laugh. "Thank you so much, doctor. I was thinking the worst. If anything bad is going to happen, it used to happen to me." She pulled me down and gave me a big hug before I left the room, and I went on to see my other patients. I needed to get it together, I could not take much more of this. Neither could my patients. Physician, first do no harm.

As I was driving home that evening, I kept replaying the day in my head. I couldn't stop thinking about how upset Sherry was. I was not happy, and it was showing to those around me. I was worrying about caring for my patients, keeping my schedule on time, maintaining the highest standards, avoiding complications, looking like I was in control, meeting high patient expectations, and being the CEO of my company. She only saw the tension and pain I was feeling, and she thought it was about her. I was tense, and it made her feel tense. The absence of my smile made her feel uneasy and nervous. As soon as I smiled, she smiled too, and the tension released for both of us. I thought about the thousands of patients I had treated and I asked myself: Was I making my patients feel good or were they feeling my unhappiness and stress?

I didn't sleep well that night. I kept hearing Sherry's voice repeating, "It's awful, isn't it…" as I tossed and turned. I felt knots in my stomach and tightness in my chest. I got up and walked around the house. I checked in on my kids as they lay sleeping, peacefully. Wrapped around their blankets and pillows going every which way, they looked so beautiful. As a proud father, I watched them take slow, sleepy breaths. I felt totally at peace in that moment.

Finally, it hit me. I had my aha moment. It was so simple, and it was right in front of me all the time. Thank you Sherry for touching my life. I was in pain. I smiled, and my pain went away. If I had only been able to share my smile with Sherry, she would have had a totally different experience.

I came to the realization that I was so focused on being an artist, surgeon, businessman, boss, father, husband, son, and all things to all people, that I had forgotten a very simple lesson in doctoring. People just need to feel good. They need relief from their pain. They want comfort from their worries, tension, and stress in their life. And they want to know that you care. If you take away someone's pain or stress, they are so grateful. I realized that smiling isn't just a part of making people look good. Smiling is Mother Nature's free facelift, it is the most attractive thing we do to our faces. Yet a smile is so much more. Smiling has the ability to make us feel good. Smiling releases our tension, and the tension of those around us.

I now know it is my duty and responsibility to share my smile and bring out the smile in my patients, in my team, and in everyone I meet. When I am being the artist-surgeon, I consummate this role by showing my smile while creating and displaying my craft. Then patients really know that they are getting my full attention, inspiration, and creativity. To help patients get their best outcomes, feel good about themselves, and build their confidence, I needed to make them smile. And the best way to get someone to smile—is to smile at them myself! That was when I started my mission to smile with everyone I ever meet. That was the birth of *The Smile Prescription*.

When I got up the next morning, I felt so much different! I was a ball full of energy, and I felt giddy. I couldn't wait to try my new outlook on my staff and patients. So before work, I looked in the mirror and I said that I am going to smile as much as I can for at least one hour. My subconscious mind kept trying to shut me down saying, "You will look stupid, you have to look professional! You already look too young, do you want people to lose respect and think of you as a silly, over-smiling, childish hippy?" But after my smile realization, I had the courage to try something new.

I walked into my office, with a big smile on my face. As I greeted my team, I told them how awesome they are and how grateful I am for their hard work. "I sincerely appreciate you choosing to be a part of the team." Immediately they looked surprised, but I continued before they could start to question me. "Moving forward, we are going to start having some fun in the office. We are going to smile and laugh more with each other, and with our patients. And we are going to start today, and have a big party for our patients!" The moment I saw their smiles and heard the laughter, I knew we were on the right track. I didn't just do the smile challenge for one hour, I did it all day long. It wasn't just for me. It was for all of my patients, my team, and everyone I came into contact with. From that day forward, life has been so much better. Something inside of me changed that day, and I embraced my gratitude and showed my appreciation for anyone who chose to be a part of my life. I never realized how simple this answer was. Smiling gives me an advantage for every challenge I face.

The day was more productive. Every day there would be unexpected problems. Now, instead of getting angry or tense, I would smile and say, "Okay, let's turn this around!" The change in the energy was palpable. My office manager, Thomas, noticed a difference and congratulated me. "The team feels your tension, and they take it personally when they don't feel their work is appreciated. Your smile uplifts the team, and for the team to open up and smile at the office makes all the difference." As we created a happier workplace, our days grew busier and our office became more successful. Smiling doesn't just make people look good. It changes what you think, how you feel, and how we treat one another.

Before my smiling revelation, there were days that I would tell the staff to smile more for our patients and for themselves, and I couldn't understand why they wouldn't listen to me. Some staff even resented being asked to smile more. So how do I make them smile now? I said it before, and I will say it again. The best way to make anyone smile is to...smile at them yourself! I was wrong when I thought my team would see me as unprofessional, and that my patients would not take me as seriously. I thought my family and friends would think my smile challenge was weird. Even though some of them did feel it was strange, they still responded with absolute positivity to my smile, and they smiled back! You too can activate your creative imagination and make your smile work for you. Start now by deciding what you would do to make yourself and other people smile as you take on the Smile Challenge. Give yourself permission to encourage your rebel, act a little crazy, and stretch your comfort zone. I dare you to try it!

Enjoy the Smile Challenge

I guarantee if you let yourself enjoy the Smile Challenge, it will have a great impact on you and others, because the power of the Smile Challenge all depends on what you put into it. Like anything else you want to be successful at, you have to work at it. The ability to change how you and those around you feel is pretty amazing, and that is why *The Smile Prescription* works. The Smile Challenge is so important because with today's technology, we have stopped communicating in a personal manner, unless you consider texting to be personal. :) Our most effective communication is with our faces. When you read someone's facial expression, you know a lot about them. Once again I say "Thank you!" to my patient Sherry, for waking me up to this powerful truth.

The Smile Challenge is Best With Smile Buddies!

Smile Buddy System

Now that you have taken on the Smile Challenge, let's play another game within a game! There is so much fun you can have with your smile, and I am here to assist you. So make it a game to find a buddy or a friend to take on the Smile Challenge with. When you find a Smile Buddy, you will get much more powerful reinforcement of your smile. Make a pinky promise that you will help each other to smile more! Here is how the Smile Buddy game works: You challenge your buddy to see who can make each other smile first, smile biggest, or laugh the loudest! You can do this with just a smile, saying something cute or funny, making faces, or just acting silly. If you are dating, this is the perfect way to build a relationship. If you are married, challenge your spouse to play the game with you. He or she is your #1 buddy! Your spouse and your family know better than anyone else when you do or do not smile. :)

The key to this game is you must create a smile that is about them and not about you. You may find something funny, but they may not be amused. Once you make your smile buddy smile or laugh, then of course you will smile and laugh too. That is what friends are for. The buddy system is a part of our DNA. You will find the buddy system used in the army, elementary school, business corporations, upper management, Alcoholics Anonymous, when you go deep sea diving, or hiking in the wilderness. Yay for the buddy system!

When we change our facial expressions from stress and tension to smiling and happy, it opens new possibilities. Let me share with you how my kids are learning in school. I know, I talk non-stop about my kids, but I can't help it, I love them and they put a smile on my face. :) They ask for my help with their homework, and of course I want to them to have everything they need. They are getting old enough that I don't have all of the answers to what they are looking for.

My smile buddies, giving me a smile workout!

But, I have an out. If I just give them the answers, do they learn anything? Of course they don't, they have to make the effort and think for themselves. And the same goes for all of us. If someone just gives us the answers for happiness and smiling and we didn't make the effort ourselves, we are still prisoners of ignorance.

The Smile Challenge and your Smile Buddy will give you the keys to release the creative mind from the captivity of our blank or frowning faces. All you have to do is start, and once you start the whole universe will work with you!

Congratulations! If you are still reading, you are AWESOME and you get an A+ because you know how important this is. You are worth it and you deserve the life of your dreams, if you are willing to work for it. You will graduate from The Smile Prescription University with honors. And, by the way, at the end of the book, you will be able to submit your request to receive The Smile Prescription certificate of completion! That is worth smiling about! :)

We are all aware that with the rapid growth of technology, people are gradually losing their ability to be personal with one another. It would seem that texting, tweeting, emails, and social media are trying to replace human face to face interaction. Here's a chance for us to use our facial expression to be an effective communicator or leader. You can't do that as an expressionless robot. Robots are amazing, though robots lack the human touch. They feel impersonal because they have no heart. We all remember in *The Wizard of Oz*, the Tin Man was robotic and just wanted to have a heart. Anything that is robotic by definition is impersonal. *The Smile Prescription* is all about giving you results and awareness in your relationships by making things more personal when we communicate effectively. What can be more personal than sharing your smile? I give you my personal guarantee (yes I am smiling) that after you finish *The Smile Prescription*, your smile will never be robotic.

More Smiling = More Personal = Longer Lasting Relationships

Less Smiling = Less Personal = Relationships Do Not Last

In my humble opinion, there is no doubt that these concepts of smiling and facial expression will make an impact in your life. You will find that the relationships you have, individually or in a group, will grow deeper and last longer when you are sharing more smiles and creating joy. So lets start! Take a look in the mirror, and show yourself the difference between a smile that is robotic, and a smile that has heart!

Smile Buddies can be everywhere. All you have to do is share with those around you, wherever you go!

This is my best facelift result ever! Just kidding... Smiling is our best facelift, and we should do this many times a day. It is free, and it is Mother Nature's way of making us more attractive.

The Smile Prescription

Will

Save

Lives

Is anything bringing your smile down?

The Smile Prescription will certainly help you personally and professionally. Yet there is so much more at stake in today's world. What is the world like today? The headlines are all bad: war, terrorists, crime, and natural disasters. You can't read the paper, watch TV, or listen to the radio without being bombarded by a myriad of negativity. *The Smile Prescription* is necessary if we are to overcome this.

I was shocked to learn that according to the World Health Organization, over 800,000 people commit suicide every year. What is worse, for each completed suicide it is estimated that there are many more attempted suicides.[6] The United States military had a staggering suicide rate of of over double the civilian rate in 2012.[7] Suicide is the tenth leading cause of death in the United States and costs $44.6 billion per year in medical bills and work loss.[8] It is incomprehensible that in the past year, more than 1 million have tried to commit suicide and 2 million have considered it. This does not even factor in the emotional pain of the family and loved ones that suffer. This is a call to all of our smile warriors out there to take action. Can you imagine what it would mean to give someone help when they most needed it? A genuine smile can truly make a difference and perhaps even save a life. How powerful is that!?!

Let me ask you a question: Have you ever been depressed, or do you know anyone who has? YOU ARE NOT ALONE! Globally, more than 350 million people suffer from depression.[9] Depression is a leading cause of disability in the world. Can you imagine the staggering number of people who cite depression as a disability, reporting that they are unable to work or support themselves and their family? One in twenty people have reported a depressive episode in the past year.[10] Depression contributes to failed relationships, divorce, poor health, weakened immune systems, and more. Depression is like a snake that squeezes the life out of people and society. We must fight back! Positive facial expression and smiling will make you bigger and stronger when facing this serpent of depression that tries to devour us. Antidepressants alone are a multi-billion dollar industry for pharmaceutical companies, yet they have not cured this problem.

I apologize for being so negative, but that is the world we live in. If this makes you feel a bit down, let's do something interesting to bring this point home. Just follow along with this exercise, and trust me, because I am a doctor. :) Just put a smile on your face and raise your hands above your head. Do this for thirty seconds and see what happens. Go ahead and try it! You will notice a difference, and if you want to heighten the experience, do this while looking in front of a mirror. The brain can only focus on so many things at one time. If your spirits are low, this exercise will change how you feel. In no way is *The Smile Prescription* intended to take the place of a physician-patient relationship. However, it is intended to help everyone raise their spirits. If you or someone you know are in need of assistance now for depression or suicidal thoughts, please call 1-800-273-8255 (1-800-273-TALK) or visit www. suicidepreventionlifeline.org.

It breaks my heart to think that there are people right now in this world thinking about taking their life. What if they had someone to smile and inspire them when they need it most? Are you going to help make a difference? We have the ability to do so, and it is so simple, yet many of us stare at life with a blank face, ignoring the power we have to uplift ourselves and those around us with our smile. These statistics on suicide and depression make me angry and sick to my stomach. To be clear, I'm not saying that smiling will cure depression or stop all suicides, though I do know that smiling can certainly help anyone in these circumstances. And, those who are depressed or contemplating suicide clearly do not smile or laugh very much or have positive facial expressions. In fact, I like to think about depression as a smile hunger, where our body and soul are starving for a smile. When we feed that hunger with smiles, our depression inevitably improves. Life should be an all-you-can-eat buffet of smiling. Let's face it, most people go through depression because life can knock you down and take the wind out of your sails. It is normal to experience depression; though it is not normal to stay there.

I love getting smile-inspiration and raising my spirits from my patients that are great smilers. One of my patients, Lisa, is in her fifties and is a proud mother of three. Lisa is a GREAT smiler! I asked her where she gets her smile from, and she told me her story, saying that she wasn't always a great smiler.

"My husband has Parkinson's disease, and he was embarrassed to go out into public because of his tremors. We had a rough couple of years after he was diagnosed. One day, my close friend asked me what was wrong because she never saw me smile.

What she said struck me, because she was right! I was upset about my life, and my face clearly showed it. So I decided to start smiling more. Since that day, I have never stopped because I love how smiling makes me feel. My smile impacts my husband and lifts him up as well. We love going out together now. My husband smiles through any trouble his tremors cause him, and we are happier than we have ever been. The positive response I received from everyone around me has been amazing! The past ten years of my life have been my smiling years. :) I knew I still had a lot to smile about because my husband was still with me, and my children were alive and healthy. I became known for my smile, and people would compliment me and talk about how I always smiled.

"I play bridge once a week, and one of the gentlemen in the group approached me one day. He said, 'I have been coming to bridge for a while now, and I am always comforted to see your smile. I lost my wife last year to cancer, and I got really depressed. And every time I saw your smile, it made me feel happy. I wanted to thank you for this as it really lifted my spirits when I needed it most!' I was so touched by this. I had no idea I could impact people this way!"

Here's another smile story that I find very funny. Scott is someone I met when I was sharing smile stories at one of my seminars. Scott shared with us a story about visiting his mother-in-law Mildred, in the United Kingdom. She asked him to walk into town to the farmer's market to buy some vegetables for dinner that night. Before they left, she pulled him aside, "Now Scott, when we walk into town, you can not wear your trainers (athletic shoes). And whatever you do, when we walk by other people, don't just smile at them like you know them. It isn't proper!" Scott got such a laugh out of this, he actually couldn't stop smiling! Then, she wouldn't let him go with her! Scott's story about smile restrictions from his mother-in-law brought the house down. Lisa and Scott are aware now of how important it is to keep smiling. Scott even has his mother-in-law Mildred smiling now too! Smiling breaks through all cultural barriers.

That is why I'm on a mission to spread the smile message. Join me in blazing this trail of smiles that today's world so desperately needs! That is my purpose as the Smile Doctor. Think of me as a cross between Patch Adams and Jack Lalanne. :) Patch Adams needs no introduction. As a physician he became famous for his charitable contributions and dressing up as a clown to make patients smile in the health-care setting. In the 1930's, Jack Lalanne started his crusade to improve the lives of others through physical fitness and exercise. Believe it or not, when Jack opened his first health studio, doctors were against him. Physicians said too much exercise and being overly muscle bound would cause heart attacks and problems with your love-life. Jack shared his message for over seventy years, inspiring millions of people to exercise their bodies and be aware of healthier foods. We all stand on the shoulders of giants, and I am here to be the smiling doctor who helps people to exercise their smiles and laugh more. It isn't that hard to be more aware of the expressions we put on our face and the meanings we give to our life. Developing your smile muscles is one of the most important exercises there is to create happiness for you and those around you! To compare smiling to Jack Lalanne's work in nutrition and health, the phrase "You are what you eat," becomes, "You are what you show on your face." :)

Bakery Smiles!

Saturday Smile

Here's a story I would like to share with you to raise awareness about smiling. So I'm feeling good because it's a Saturday morning. :) My wife and daughter like to sleep in so I pack my noisy boys into the car to go get breakfast. My dad used to bring us doughnuts on Saturdays, so I can't help but take the kids to the bakery. We are in the car, and it is a little too early in the morning for the boys to really get into their fighting (if you have kids you understand), and I propose a game to keep them occupied.

I put my best smile on, "Hey you guys, want to play a game?"

"What is it?" they say with excitement.

"As we drive, let's watch these people walking and exercising. Let's see how many we can count that have a smile on their face!"

"Okay!" they say with the energy like we were going to Disney World. If they were dogs their tails would be wagging like crazy. It may just be the thought of pastries getting their blood sugars up, but I will take what I can get. We look at

37

the walkers, runners, bikers, and stroller-pushing pedestrians. One, two, three, and so on.

"Do you see any smiling faces?" I say.

"No Dad..." Not a single smile. "Wait a minute...that kid tripped over and fell into the bushes, so his sister started laughing at him." On a beautiful, sunny Saturday morning in Florida, in a picturesque neighborhood with trees and golf greens, only the sister with the clumsy brother was smiling.

We get all the way to the bakery, passing at least thirty people. "I wonder why people don't smile more." My kids and I ponder. The facial expressions of choice were neutral, downward gazes, or mildly pained. We walk into the bakery smiling, with a sense of adventure as we count faces (my kids were more focused on the doughnuts). People were there, eating, drinking coffee, reading the paper, listening to classical music overhead, and chatting. The young girl behind the counter had a slight smile ready for us. Everyone else was looking downward at their food, newspaper, or electronic gadget of choice. All of the other workers were moving like robots: cleaning, organizing, preparing, working, doing something, being busy, but not smiling. No one looked like they were having fun or enjoying life. I call it robot-face, or bot-face for short.

We walk up to the counter to give our order. I have a soft smile (a.k.a. the micro-smile, keep reading to learn more) as my boys order, and they can be so wiggly as they talk—you know how little kids somehow cannot just stand still? They are being so cute that the teenage girl behind the counter starts smiling even bigger. Now we are getting somewhere!

I smile and tell her, "Hey, we've been people watching today to see who is smiling, and you are the only one in the store that has a smile on their face—and you have a GREAT smile!" She immediately breaks out into a great big smile and says, "Thank you!" What a nice gift she gave us with her smile!

I told her, "Keep smiling, and make sure you share it with everyone!" As I put the change in the tip jar, she laughed and said, "Thank you for the tip!"

"No problem," I said.

She looked at me and said, "No, the tip about smiling. You are right, I do need to smile more. I don't want to look like a zombie. That is a tip that I can use all the time!" And she gave me her biggest smile yet.

We all enjoyed a smile together, and our morning was a memorable one.

It certainly made my boys happy, though I'm not sure if it was the smiling, the pastries, or the sugary sprinkles on top (sprinkles somehow make us smile too).

What Is the Point of Smiling So Much?

My family loves to make ourselves (and other people) smile by joking around and goofing off. People we don't even know look at us and smile as we have fun and horse around, inevitably embarrassing my wife and daughter. We become friends and make conversation out of nothing with people that were strangers to us a few moments prior. Just the other day, I was walking through the department store with my two boys, and we were sharing our smiles. The first three people we walked by immediately started smiling. We walked by a gentleman in the DVD section, and he saw my kids get so excited about the movies he actually broke out into laughter. Some would have been offended, but I was just happy he was smiling and laughing. I have nothing to be embarrassed about. He apologized, "I'm sorry, I think of my kids when I see them looking at the movies, they are such a handful!" I told him, "I know, isn't it great? We have plenty to smile about!" Whether they are smiling with us or smiling at us, who cares? We just want to make more smiles and laughter in this world.

I was shocked to realize that so many people walk around with a blank face, so I started counting to see if I was just fooling myself. I have counted smiles in grocery stores, parks, shopping malls, theaters, restaurants, airports, popular theme parks, indoors, and outdoors. Out of a hundred, the most common number of smiling faces I count is three!! The highest I got was ten, and that was in a restaurant when people were really yucking it up (was it the wine?). A survey of 2,000 people showed that adults smile on average seven times per day.[11]—REALLY?!?

One of the reasons we may not recognize this lack of smiling is because it is socially inappropriate to look at people's faces when they are not addressing us. Just consider if you are glancing around the room and someone makes eye-contact while you are looking at them. We often divert our eyes and look the other way to avoid embarrassment. So, even if someone is wearing a blank face, it is almost a reflex for us not to check out their face too much. We don't want to be rude! These social rules makes us less aware of how many people wear flat faces in their daily activities.

I have a question for you. Have you ever noticed how many (or how few) people are smiling around you? Or how often YOU smile through the course of a day? When I ask people how many smiles they think they will see in the next hundred people they come across, some say as high as seventy-five percent! Most of us tend to overestimate how much other people (and ourselves) smile. When you realize that so few people smile during their daily activities, it is not so surprising that stress and depression are such a problem today.

Smile training with my Smile Buddies! We must practice our smile if we want to be good at it!

Now, consider the opposite of this blank-faced scenario. What if we walked around with a BIG smile on our face? What if we are just happy to be alive, happy we are not in the hospital, or happy that we have two hands, and we show this on our face with a grateful grin? People will think there is something wrong with us, or that we are drunk, or up to something! It should be the other way around! The world would be a better place if more people walked around with smiling faces, and there were fewer flat expressions to be seen. Is it just me?!?

Living In Captivity

Taking the Smile Challenge and making Smile Buddies will allow you to see things much differently. For example, take a moment to think about the simple things we do on a daily basis. If you go to the gym, there are usually some very motivated people there working out early in the morning. Their drive is admirable, though their faces don't usually look very happy. We go to the grocery store, surrounded by more choice and abundance than most of the world has ever seen. Even though there are hundreds of high quality foods to choose from, none of this makes people smile as they are shopping. People seem to be very busy and occupied as they push their carts and look so serious, perusing their shopping list of bananas, deodorant, and ice cream. There appears to be a great lack of happiness in this supermarket paradise.

You can see walkers, joggers, and skaters all seemingly unaware of the joyful perspective that they are not crippled. They have the ability to run and move their healthy bodies. As we described earlier, the facial expression of choice appears to be flat and expressionless, with a hint of pain or wincing. Even families walking together often seem unhappy. Moms and dads, strolling around with their precious children like ducklings in a picture perfect moment, yet they appear sober and mechanical as they walk along, which doesn't make you feel very warm on the inside. It's as if our society is on the autopilot mode and we watch life as it goes by.

I'm holding my brother in captivity :) Hee Hee!

The hypnosis of daily activities can make us look like we are automatons, or on cruise control. We can appear devoid of joy, happiness, or gratitude for the blessings we have. The bottom line is, people don't tend to look that happy, even though we live with some of the greatest financial, technological, and informational abundance in the history of the world! People often look like they are living in captivity. When we go to the zoo, we sometimes feel bad for the animals and say, "Wow, those animals

41

don't look that happy." Yet, the animals in the zoo look through the bars at the humans and say, "Wow, those people don't look that happy." Who is the one living in captivity?!? Maybe that is why it makes us so sad when we feel for the animals at the zoo. On some level, most of us know what it means to be restricted, constrained, or held back from what we really need. People are held captive in their minds from what they want most—to smile and be happy. Are you going to take control of your life, or are you going to live in the captivity of the auto-pilot mind? Break through the bars, take the Smile Challenge to heart, find your Smile Buddies, and claim the freedom, happiness, and smiling in your life now!

Do you see people that look like they live in captivity?

Are you looking at me? Who is the one in captivity now?!?

"As a visual society, people treat us differently based on how young or how old they think we are. We are also treated differently based on how much or how little we smile. The most important person that treats us differently based on our smiling is ourselves. I call this "smil-ism" or "face-ism" and you can not deny that it exists, though you can use it to your advantage."

—Dr. Rich

Smile as If Your Life Depends on It, BECAUSE IT DOES!

So let's take action and not be the victims of a learned, blank-faced culture. We can absolutely choose freedom and happiness by consciously and intentionally using our facial appearance and our smile. When we focus on helping ourselves and others smile more, we increase our quality of life and productivity. There is a tremendous lack of smiling and happiness in this world, and every smile we create counts! Everything in life is made up of relationships, and one of the most valuable things in any relationship is how we share our joy through smiles and laughter.

Good luck fellow Smile Warriors, the battle ahead will be a fun one when you take the Smile Challenge and work with Smile Buddies. Smiling makes life more meaningful and fulfilling. Let's use the power of smiling to lift up ourselves and those around us. So heads up, hands up, smiles on, have fun, and let's get started!

Are you ready for the thrill of your life?

"How and why you smile shows how you live your life. When you see, hear, or feel what makes someone smile, you learn a lot about their strengths, weaknesses, and what they really are looking for."

— Dr. Rich

People are reading *The Smile Prescription* many times over because of the impact this content can have in your life. Make no mistake, your smile will be tested, and in fact, you will be tested multiple times on this every day for the rest of your life. Every time you interact with another person (or look at yourself), someone's brain is going to judge you on how happy, confident, trustworthy, and capable you are. Will you get a good grade on that test? My job is to make sure you get an "A+" because you are worth it! The world will always challenge us, and *The Smile Prescription* gives you all the tools you need. It is up to you to use them.

And next comes the rules for *The Smile Prescription*! If you NEED to achieve more smiling and happiness for yourself, your family, and your work, you MUST:

1. **Give yourself permission** to go all out in this game and give it all that you have—you will only get out of it what you put into it. Give yourself the freedom and flexibility to GET EXCITED and ENJOY what facial expression and smiling have to offer. If you play in the Super Bowl with a

45

casual attitude, you most certainly will not win. And if you walk into the stadium knowing that you are a champion and you are going to win, your chances of bringing home the trophy change dramatically. This is what we refer to this as "getting your adrenaline up," as this is what makes us most engaged. You will perform some uncomfortable facial expressions, though I promise you will not break your face. :) Go with the flow and see how far you can push yourself. You will be surprised at what you will find!

2. **Believe in *The Smile Prescription*** and suspend your disbelief until you reach the end of the book. Said another way, believe everything this book says, agree and perform the exercises. After you finish the book, then you can allow your inner skeptic to poke as many holes as possible. You will find that the power of smiling holds up against any criticism. Smiling and facial expressions will change your life when used correctly and frequently. People often doubt a statement before they hear the end of the sentence—and that would be a shame if they missed the messages in this book. Einstein said that what prevented him from learning is his own education. Do you have anything that prevents you from learning? If you hear nay-saying voices in your head, simply befriend them and ask them if they can cut you some slack. Keep them at bay until you can go through the whole book and then let them have their say after you can fully digest the book. At the end of this book (or right now), you will be a believer.

3. **Have Fun**! Which isn't hard to do when you are smiling! Are you smiling right now? Make it a game you like to play, and the work will seem easy. Good, keep it up, turn the page, and let's get started and see what the research tells us in Chapter two! I love this chapter, keep reading, doctor's orders. :)

Congratulations for making it this far! If you want even more benefit and value from *The Smile Prescription*, you must step out of your comfort zone. It is easier to do than you think. And in the next chapter, we will show you the science to prove it! Can you imagine researchers standing around in their laboratories, wearing lab coats, lighting Bunsen burners and setting up equipment, performing studies and research on…SMILES?!? Well, you better believe it, because not only did they do the research, they found results that will absolutely improve your health, longevity, and quality of life, so let's get to it! I'll see you in the next chapter!

DOCTOR'S ORDERS:

1. Remind yourself to be more aware of who is and is not smiling.

2. Consider who in your life needs to smile and laugh more?

3. Research has proven the power of smiling. Are you using this to your advantage or disadvantage?

4. What are your reasons for wanting to smile more?

5. Be prepared to have a lot less stress, more fun, and greater successes!

6. Take the Smile Challenge with your Smile Buddy!

SMILE REFLECTIONS:

- Why did you pick up this book? What are you looking for?

- How would you rate your happiness on a scale of 1 to 10?

- Who do you want to see smile the most in your life?

- Who are the people that want to see *you smile* the most?

"I wish I had your optimism, Ted."

chapter two

SMILE FASTER, BETTER, LONGER, AND STRONGER

"Smile for no reason and inspire wonder for those who pass by"
— Dr. Rich

The real man smiles in trouble, gathers strength from distress, and grows brave by reflection.—Thomas Paine

Are you excited to hear what the "Smiling Scientists" have come up with in their laboratories? I can see them now, groups of people congregating, smiling, engaging in deep conversation with special lights, glass containers everywhere, and the pouring of special liquids—or wait, maybe I am seeing the bartender at happy hour? Either way, as long as they are smiling, they are on track. :) So congratulations on making it this far, I promise that your smile will never be the same! Can you tell how it's working already? Smiling is the facial expression of choice, and this chapter reveals the latest in smile research and other facial expressions. Doesn't the word "research" make you want to smile?! OK, scientific investigations may not automatically trigger happiness in all of us, but after reading these simple yet mind-blowing studies, the research actually *WILL* make you smile and reinforce your understanding of why your smile is so important. :)

Nose wrinkles are the sign of a great smile!

"Hi, you must be the new guy."

After you complete this chapter, you should be able to confidently walk into any university, hang out at the water cooler, and go toe to toe with top PhD's, researchers, and scientists about the study of smile, a.k.a. *Smilology*. So are you ready to get educated and scientific about your smile, with just a few pages of effort? In this chapter, we will discuss relevant scientific findings that agree with our smile hypothesis, which is:

Proactive, genuine smiling will increase happiness, the quality of relationships, health, longevity, and emotional resilience.

This research is the foundation of our five-step smile process that we start in Chapter three, so it is important that you read through these studies in the order presented. While I was putting all of this research together, a funny thing happened to me that I want to share.

Taxi Driver

I attended an event in California for authors and experts to gather and share their message with a larger audience. I met the most wonderfully interesting people from all over the world, including professional athletes, business coaches, relationship experts, entertainers, CEO's, stay-at-home parents, financial experts, marketing executives, professional pilots, and even horse whisperers. Everyone there had the common focus of creating more value in the lives of others around their field of expertise. There were so many wonderful experiences we had, I felt giddy knowing I made friends that I would keep for a lifetime. And the best was yet to come!

As I was leaving the event, I shared a cab to the airport with a couple that owned a weight loss business. I thought to myself that smiling must be critical for their business, as they have a lot of clients dealing with self-image issues and depression. Not to mention they provide customer service, which does not exist without a smile. So as we get to know each other in the taxi, they ask me what I do. I was in the front seat of the cab, and as I start talking about the power of smiling, I tried to include the taxi driver in our discussion. He must like to smile, right? Unfortunately, I wasn't getting a positive vibe from him as I spoke, so I gently guided my conversation to the back of the cab. The driver seemed more focused on the road, and I didn't want to be rude by talking at him. After all, our lives were in his hands. :)

So we talked about how smiling impacts the weight loss industry and shared a lot of great ideas. We exchanged information, and they left the cab at their gate to fly back home. My stop was coming next, so it was just the driver and me for a few minutes. He didn't seem to be engaged by the smile conversation, so I changed the subject. "So, are you just getting started today, or are you finishing up your shift?"

He still seemed like his presence was distant as he gazed ahead, "Yes, I am finishing up soon." He kept driving as if he preferred the silence to conversation. After more than a brief pause, he goes on to say, with a completely blank face, "Yeah, you know…I really should smile more often."

Where did that come from?!? My heart melted for this person who so gently confessed that he needed more smiling, yet he had not told his face! I didn't lose anytime and said, "Yeah, it feels good right? And we like to see our families smile, right?" Now I've got him smiling, and he is nodding his head. "And the best way to do that…is to smile ourselves!"

"Yes, you are right. My kids are great smilers, they are always smiling!" His smile was fully engaged as he began to open up and talk about his family that he obviously loved.

He drove up to my gate and helped me with my luggage. I wished him a safe drive home, and he said to me, "Keep smiling!" And he waved goodbye. What a wonderful friend I met. We may be on different paths in life, have different backgrounds, different families, and differ in age or culture. Yet we all share the same power of a smile, that can impact our lives and bring us closer to one another.

Chopstick Smile Improves Stress Response— Grin and Bear it

My family loves eating Asian food, and we have a lot of fun watching my kids use—or try to use—their chopsticks. As we were giving our order at a restaurant, the waitress was smiling at my kids as they were playing and holding the chopsticks in their teeth. We had a lot of fun with this, because when the kids have the chopsticks between their teeth, they don't talk as much, it is harder for them to fight with each other, and it brings joy to our family and everyone around us. I had no idea researchers were studying how this same technique of putting chopsticks between your teeth can make a physical change inside of us and reduce our stress. After trying to control our very active kids at dinner, my wife and I needed some chopsticks-in-our-teeth therapy.

So how did this study work? Researchers from the University of Kansas[1] put together a study using 170 college students. I'm not surprised this study came from KU because their mascot "Big Jay" certainly has a nice smile. :) The students were divided into three groups: those with a neutral expression, a fake smile, and a genuine smile. How do you tell a fake smile from a genuine smile? You will always know because you will feel it. A real smile radiates authenticity and shows in the eyes because your eye muscles contract. This type of a smile is also called "squinching" or "smizing." I love those names. It makes me laugh and smile just talking about it. Try it for yourself and demonstrate in the mirror to see how it works. Trust your insight, your inner detective will always tell you the truth. You will also see how a fake smile does not close the eye muscles as much as a genuine smile, and it does not feel as good either. The fancy, scientific name for the genuine smile (using the eyes) is called a "Duchenne" smile, and the fake smile is called a "Non-Duchenne" smile if you absolutely must know. :)

This demonstrates a genuine smile, activating both the eyes (squinching or smizing) and the mouth.

53

A fake smile activates only the mouth and not the eyes.

Getting back to the KU study, the students were coached on how to hold the correct smile for their group, neutral, genuine, or fake. The genuine smile group were shown how to hold chopsticks in their back teeth, smile widely, and squint their eyes. The fake smile group were trained to hold the chopsticks in their front teeth and activate only the smiling muscles without squinting the eyes. The neutral group was taught to hold the chopsticks in their teeth with a relaxed face (see photos below). Participants were then given two tasks to perform. The first task was to trace a star with their non-dominant hand while viewing only the mirror image. To make it even more stressful, a loud obnoxious sound was given if they drew outside the lines. The second task included placing their hand in ice water for one minute. Both of these stressful tasks elevated the subject's heart rate, and this was

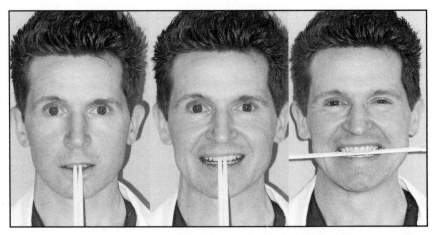

Examples of neutral group (left), fake smile group (middle), and genuine smile group (right).

monitored during the recovery immediately after the task was completed. Chopsticks were held in the mouth only during the period of completing the tasks, and not during the recovery period. Researchers were measuring the stress response of the subjects by monitoring how high the heart rate would go and how quickly it would return to normal as they recovered. Can you guess what their findings were?

The results show that recovery from the stressful event was quicker and heart rates were the lowest for the students in the genuine smile group, followed by slower recoveries in the fake smile group. The neutral group (non-smiling) had the slowest recovery and the highest heart rate of all the groups. So when we are performing stressful tasks, like trying to recover a deleted show on the DVR, getting the kids to school on time, or reaching for that drink at the bottom of the ice cooler, remember that putting a smile on your face WILL decrease your stress! These chopstick findings can for make a great game for your next house-party. Give everyone chopsticks, and let the games begin! The bottom line is: when we have stress in our lives, which we all do, putting a genuine smile on your face will help you feel better more quickly, even if you have to use chopsticks to do it. :)

Pen-In-Mouth Smile Study

If you don't have chopsticks handy, a pen or pencil will also do the trick! I know it may be too much, but for even more proof, I'm going to mention one more similar study (the nerd inside of me loves facts and this is important so I wanted to share it with you). And once you start smiling, people are going to want to know what is so different and what has changed about you. This will give you more to talk about when you share your smile with others. So here we go. This next study measured how placing a pen in your teeth changes how funny things seem to you. They also used three control groups, this time from 92 University of Illinois undergraduate students. These groups were similar to those in the chopstick study. One group put the pen in their back teeth to mimic a genuine smile, the next group held the pen in their lips to inhibit a smile, and the last group held the pen in their hand as a control for a neutral face.

Next, they rated the funniness of four Gary Larson "Far Side" cartoons on a scale of 0 to 9. The cartoons were pre-rated as being moderately funny, a 6.6 on a 9 point funniness scale. I am a HUGE Gary Larson fan, please do not tell him that his brilliant and hilarious comics were only rated 6.6 on a scale of 9! The researchers were able to demonstrate that putting a pen in the teeth and mimicking a genuine smile did make subjects rate the cartoons as more funny. Holding the pen in the lips and blocking a smile yielded the lowest funniness ratings, and holding the pen in the non-dominant hand gave a neutral rating.

So if you want your next joke to go over better, have everyone put a pen in their teeth (not touching their lips) before you deliver the punchline. Or you can ask them to say "Waikiki" or "cheese" as it mimics the same motion without using the pen, and requires the same activation of the smile muscles. Thank you to these scientists for performing studies that many people think are crazy or silly. These results validate to us that smiling *does* work and is powerful! I bet those students in the genuine smile group didn't even realize that they were starting their own Smile Challenge as they participated in these studies :) Change your face and you will change your feelings. I wonder if this works when breaking bad news, "Mom and Dad, I need to tell you about my report card, but before I do please put this pen in your teeth. Just trust me on this one." :)

Facial Feedback Hypothesis - Say What?!?

Did you know your smile muscles are the STRONGEST muscles in your entire body? Even if you are able to break the world record deadlift and lift over 1,155 pounds, this will never compare with how your smile muscles can lift up thousands or millions or even billions of people!

Your smile muscles are powerful beyond compare, and isn't it great that we don't need chopsticks or pens or heavy weights to tap into this mighty force right under our nose? Scientists and researchers have known about the power of smiling for a long time now. Even the great naturalist, Charles Darwin, wrote about the power of facial feedback in the nineteenth century. You probably remember Darwin from your high school studies as the father of evolution. His theories were so controversial at the time, the church spoke out a great deal against his teachings (they apologized 200 years later). Darwin wrote about the Facial Feedback Hypothesis. Do we really need a complicated term like this to tell us that smiling is powerful? At the end of the day, this complicated name states that facial expressions can enhance or suppress our emotional responses.

It seems like common sense. It is hard to be excited at a party when having a dull and flat face, just as it is hard to be bored when your face is very expressive and animated. Don't you think so? Your facial expression is tied to your emotions, or as we like to say:

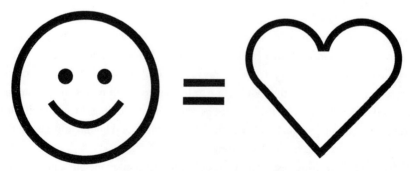

Your Face = Your Feelings

So what does "Your Face = Your Feelings" mean? Think about it this way. If you are having a party, do you invite people that like to smile and make you smile? If someone never smiles, we call them a party-pooper, a killjoy, or a wet blanket, and we don't invite them to the party. Or if we do invite them, we try to get them to smile. Flat faces bring us down. If we invite people who love to smile and make others smile, we call them the life of the party! Well guess what? Life is a party, and you are invited! It is a BYOS party—Bring Your Own Smile. So lets party on! And let me share with you as a facial plastic surgeon how the difference between the smilers and frowners at the party all comes down to the battle of the facial muscles.

Battle of the Brow

Your facial muscles are constantly battling to determine how you feel! So why is it that only a few people have a smile on their face at any given time? Is it because the frown muscles are bullying too many faces out there? Are the smile muscles just not strong enough to overcome the stress and tension of the day? It always makes me smile when I hear people say, "It takes more muscles to frown than it does to smile." First of all, I love any sentiment that encourages smiling. However, if you are smiling really big, you can use a heck of a lot more muscles than when someone frowns. And when you say it takes more muscles to frown, it is almost as if we are saying people are lazy and only take the path of least resistance! "Well, I would frown, but that takes too many muscles, so I guess I'll just smile instead..." Bottom line, *The Smile Prescription* will show you that using your smile muscles is powerful and easy to do.

Reading about frowning brings my face down! Can we smile yet?!?

But what would happen if we knock out some of those frown muscles or muscles that show tension? Does your smile get stronger? This is exactly what some people are doing with Botox®. Yeah, yeah, I know you are thinking this is why celebrities look so funny. However, when performed correctly, Botox® can actually make you feel better. :) In fact, a study has been performed in the U.K.[2] that showed when you block some of the frown muscles, people demonstrated consistently higher mood scores. No wonder Botox® is one of the highest satisfaction cosmetic treatments in the country. Botox® assists you in beating the bully at the "battle of the brow."

And smiling is the most natural Botox® you can get because when we activate our smile muscles, it automatically relaxes our frown muscles and forehead muscles. You can't have a "furrowed brow" when you are wearing a genuine smile. Did you ever realize that you can't really flex your smile and frown muscles at the same time? Look in the mirror or on your camera-phone and give it a try if you really want to have fun with your face! You can smile, and you can frown...but when you try to do both at the same time, it just crumples up your whole face! Great selfie material. :)

This is very powerful because it means you can control your feelings by controlling how you move your face and flex your facial muscles. You may feel furious on the inside, but if you choose to have a flat face, or dare I say even a smile, it will mess up your ability to get really angry and upset. This brings us to one of the core truths in *The Smile Prescription*, and I believe it to be one of the greatest challenges this book has to offer:

The time we need to smile the most is when we want to smile the least. — Dr. Rich

When you are upset, depressed, angry, fearful, nervous, uncomfortable, or embarrassed, the battle of the muscles on your brow is raging and you usually don't feel like smiling. These emotions are important signals to us that we need to pay attention to. But what happens if we stay with the negative emotions too long? We know what happens if we let ourselves wallow in negativity. Do you know the best way to break out of these pessimistic patterns of feeling that we all go through? That is right. Put a smile on your face, and it will break the pattern. The battle of the brow is a hard fought war, and those who endure will create more happiness for themselves and those around them. **Life is tough. Your Smile is Tougher.**

Suddenly Maude regretted getting botox.

There was a powerful study performed in Sweden[3] on the "battle of the brow." They demonstrated that it is indeed hard to frown at a smiler, and hard to smile at a frowner. We may know this intuitively, yet think about what this means on a deeper level. If you are smiling, you make it hard for people around you to make you frown or to be mean to you. How valuable would that be for you? And, if you frown, you are now making it harder for people to smile at you or to make you smile. Is that what you really want? Keep smiling, avoid frowning, and know that your smile is a powerful warrior and defender of your emotions, feelings, and happiness. In this smile war, those who strike hard and fast with their genuine smile consistently beat their frown to the punch.

You wouldn't hit a guy with glasses, would you? Or would you hit a guy with a smile on their face? What about someone with smiling glasses on ?!?

Master Your Brow

Our brow and facial expressions are important if we want to win the battle for controlling our happiness and taking charge in our lives. We must take control of our facial muscles. :) A furrowed brow means tension, and that can be helpful when we need it. But a perpetually furrowed brow means trouble. I love talking about how my patient Shelley mastered her brow and facial expressions, making her life something beyond what she has ever dreamed.

I always think about my patient "Smiling Shelley" when I talk about how smiling makes us feel better and changes our mood. When I see Shelley in the office, she greets me with a big beautiful smile that shows her back teeth as she gives me a bear hug. Her smile is so big it looks like she ate a banana sideways. Every time I see her she tells me about her grandkids and shares pictures and videos on her phone. Shelley has been coming to me for years, and she is truly one of the most positive people I have ever met. Her husband Bob doesn't always come, though when he does it is definitely a party. One day I asked, "Shelley, I'm curious, you are always smiling and so happy, do you mind if I ask what makes you smile so much?"

She said, "It's the only way to be! I've been through so much in my life, I've got too much to be happy about to be any other way." I was shocked by what she said next. "I was abused as a teenager, and I got pregnant with my daughter. In those days, you didn't go to college when you were pregnant, but I did. I had a lot of support from my family, and my professors looked after me and helped out when I needed it. It was so amazing, when I graduated, my class pitched in and bought me a VW Bug that they all signed on the hood. I cried so much that day, I was so grateful. I just kept my faith and I kept smiling because it made me feel better when I felt hopeless and depressed! Now I have three beautiful grandchildren and a wonderful husband. Why shouldn't I smile? Now look at these pictures, wouldn't you smile too?"

I was so humbled that she would share such a deep moment with me. She gave her story so freely. It makes me aware that by facing our challenges with a smile, it helps us move beyond the painful moments in life, no matter how deep the wounds are. Whatever makes us upset or puts us in a grouchy mood would not compare with what Shelley has been through. We are human, and it is okay to be grouchy, upset, anxious, or depressed sometimes. Though it is not okay to stay there and wallow in the pain. Just think about Shelley's story of uncommon hardship. Shelley's struggle inspires us to find the gratitude in our life, and it is never too late to do this and realize how much abundance there is in our world. All you have to do to understand this is smile *right now*. Go ahead, give yourself permission to smile, just like Shelley!

Einstein said you can live a life as if nothing is a miracle, or as if everything is a miracle. Have you recognized the miracles or wins in your life? I don't know about you, but it always seems that we have more in our lives worth smiling about that we realize! I try to think about the blessings and miracles in my life all the time, and it always puts a smile on my face when I turn my focus from the negative to the positive.

Scowling affects how we feel):

Frowning = Frosty

Okay, so what happens to your face when you roll back time and look at your wins? If what you are focusing on makes you smile, you are doing a great job! If what you are focusing on crumples your brow (tension) or freezes your face (expressionless or frosty), then we need to work a little harder to thaw you out! When you activate smiling muscles, you know it elevates your mood and enhances stress recovery. Try it for yourself and see. When we defeat frowning muscles and win the battle of the brow, we will raise our spirits. So does that mean breaking or weakening our smiling muscles (flattening our facial expression) will bring down our mood? Yes, it absolutely does lower our spirits when we flatten our facial expression. Frowning makes us feel frosty. Just ask Smiling Shelley. Now please forgive me, I know I like to get technical with the science and research, but I can't help it because people need to smile more. See for yourself if this isn't valuable information from the University of Pittsburgh.[4] They demonstrated that those with the weakest smile muscles have higher levels of depression, while those with moderately weak smiles have lower levels of depression. Can you imagine? We had better get our smiles moving if we know what is good for us!

What if I told you that depression is higher in people who have a behavioral limitation (rather than a physical limitation) on their ability to smile? A behavioral limitation would mean we do not choose to smile, even when we actually have a lot to smile about. That is sad, isn't it? If you look around, there are many people that make the choice of not smiling, because we are bombarded with negativity, even when surrounded with abundance. I would predict that this behavioral limitation can and will increase the risk of depression. Simply put, smiling makes us happy, and frowning makes us sad. Can we use this to help when we feel depressed? Yes. Time and time again, research confirms that our face equals our feelings. So if a credit card advertisement asks, "What's in your wallet?" *The Smile Prescription* asks, "What's on your face?"

What is a self-conscious smile?

Self-Conscious Selfie

Let me tell you a story about when I was a kid. I broke my front tooth, and I have never felt so self-conscious about anything in my life. I still remember trying to hide it from my mom. She noticed immediately that something was wrong when I covered my mouth with my hand and wouldn't smile around her. I laugh now as I remember all the funny things I did because I felt I had something to hide. Thankfully, my dad was a dentist, and he always made sure my teeth were taken care of. He fixed my tooth right away and it put the smile back on my face. Maybe that is why I like to smile so much! But I learned something important that day. I realized how powerful a smile can be, and *how painful it is not to smile!* Even though my tooth was broken, I still had the same ability to smile. The difference was that I was so concerned what other people would think about me, that I refused to allow myself to smile. And it was agonizing!

> *"Anything that takes our smile away has some degree of pain. Choosing to smile will lessen our pain and make us feel better."* — Dr. Rich

The funny thing is, ever since I started writing *The Smile Prescription*, I had never before realized how many people are self-conscious about their smile. You probably know people like this too, or maybe this is you. Some people feel they have bad teeth, or they say smiling gives them wrinkles. Sometimes, they just have low self-confidence. What a terrible tragedy not to enjoy your smile!

When people come into my office, they do it because they want to look and feel better about themselves. One of the first things I do is ask people to smile in the mirror. Why? Because it is the most attractive thing we do to our face. A smile is Mother Nature's free facelift, and we don't want to fool with Mother Nature! A smile is a magnet that "attracts" other people to us. And heck, it just feels good to do! I was amazed when I found there are people that have a very hard time smiling at themselves in the mirror. Some people, no matter what happens to them, they find a way to smile all the time! And some people, no matter what happens, they find reasons to never smile. Do you know what I mean? That is just the way some people are. It is almost as if there are people out there with a debilitated smile. These people rarely smile, their smile is weak, and even when they want to smile, it is restricted because they are self-conscious about how they look. That is exactly how I was when my tooth was broken. Look around, there are more than a few people out there like this. The good news is, there is hope, and anyone who wants to smile more certainly can.

Here's an example of what I'm talking about. Whenever someone comes into my office, the first thing my staff does is take pictures. Any of my patients will tell you that we love taking pictures. We want to be able to reveal before and after results. We take photos of patients when they are smiling. We absolutely love bringing out and enhancing someone's smile. I found it interesting one day when a patient didn't want to smile for the camera.

He complained, "I don't feel comfortable smiling, I always take weird pictures when I smile. When I try to smile for the camera, I can never do it right!"

"What do you mean?" I asked.

"I try to smile when they say 'cheese!' though I never make a good smile! I always look goofy or weird. That's why I don't do it!"

Here is what I told him, "Okay, let's take this picture, and I want you to *attack the camera!* What I mean by this is that you need to sit up straight, square your shoulders, lean your head forward, and break out a big smile. And I want you to do one more thing."

"What is it?" he said.

"I want you, inside your head or out loud, to say 'I don't give a *DAMN* what people think about me!'"

In a split-second, out comes this genuine smile, almost to the verge of laughter. No hesitation, no awkward smile, I only see a real smile. It seemed like not caring what others think about him felt really good! When we don't care what other people think about us, it is really difficult to make a fake or strained smile.

The facts are that we have the power to change and control the meaning we give to our actions and our smile. The meanings we choose for our life will allow us to control our level of wellbeing. If we choose to focus on how we are empowered, we will feel greater freedom. If we decide to focus on our limitations, we will feel imprisoned. It gives me great joy, and in fact, I love it when patients come in and they brag about how they feel. It becomes a party in the office and we all start cheering for them because we are making a difference in their lives. What is amazing is that they didn't need me to be able to brag about their appearance. They could have done that before they ever walked through my door. My job is to show them that they are beautiful before and after their treatments. So here is a powerful exercise you can do right now. Just look in the mirror, and see for yourself how much better a smile will make our face look! Nothing we do to our face will ever look as good as what our smile can do for us!

Mother Theresa was not considered to be a runway model, but when she smiled, the whole world smiled with her. It's like a game. You look in the mirror, put a smile on your face, and look for things to brag about. I know, some of you may be saying, "Well that doesn't work for me, I have nothing to smile about." Or you say, "It feels phony when I smile because nothing is going right for me." I understand where you are coming from. Let's just suppose you did have things to smile about. Do it, and see what happens! It is all about taking charge of you, and allowing yourself to stretch your comfort zone. When you shave or put on makeup in the morning and get ready, the main thing we are in control of is how we express ourselves. Are you choosing to express yourself with or without a smile? When you get dressed, put on a good attitude and smile. Let your smile out and see if you have a smile that is playful, flirty, mischievous, or even naughty! Before you know it, your smile will become more powerful and real. The more you see your inner and outer beauty, the more it makes you smile.

Here is a great quote from Shakespeare:

"There is nothing good or bad, but thinking makes it so."

The Smile Prescription version of that quote is:

"There is nothing good or bad, but smiling or frowning makes it so."

What is good or bad only comes from the meaning we give. Smiling (and frowning) changes the meaning we give to things. The more we smile, the more good we see. The less we smile, the more bad we see. As I said before, some people will smile no matter what happens to them. Some people will not smile, no matter what happens to them. The difference between these two types of people is the meaning (thinking) and the smiling they give to their lives. Do we really have to think this much about things to put a smile on our face? Really?!?

Forced or Fake Smile

Now that you have bragged a bit about your smile and have a better idea of what makes you smile, can you feel your smile muscles getting stronger? You will feel your cheeks getting bigger, but don't worry, they won't get too big. :) It is a little different than building muscles in the gym, your clothes will still fit just fine, even when your smile muscles are bulging. :) Besides, a smile goes with any outfit of any size. So while we are practicing and growing our ability to smile, what if someone accuses us of faking our smile? I have had people ask me, "What if someone asks me to smile and I don't feel like it? If I have to give a fake smile, it doesn't feel good at all!" This is a real concern for some people so we can address that now.

One of the definitions of a "fake smile" is when we care too much about what other people think about us. If you don't care what others think about you, there is no such thing as a fake smile. You just smile whenever you want to. Now a fake smile is better than no smile at all, when your attitude is good. That is why "fake it till you make it" is a good thing, when our attitude is good. Any smile when you have a bad attitude will usually result in negativity. I applaud anyone putting a smile on their face when they don't feel like smiling because they are believing in a greater purpose. Just putting chopsticks in your teeth, like we talked about earlier in the chapter, will create great feelings inside and build your smile muscles. When you smile or laugh so hard until your facial muscles are getting sore, then you know your smile is growing. :)

Fake smiling (excluding the eyes) shows a lower wellbeing when performed frequently, and a higher wellbeing when performed infrequently.

You can always see and feel the difference between a fake and real smile when you pay attention and are present in the moment.

Take a look at kids when they are playing. They are having fun and are not self-conscious, and they don't know what a fake smile is. If little kids run around and don't mind that their noses and faces need to be cleaned, they certainly won't care what people think about their smile. That self-awareness comes when we are teenagers and peer pressure teaches us that smiling like a kid isn't so cool. Do you remember those days? Being a teen can be difficult because the opinions of others are so important at that stage in our lives. We may put on a fake smile for our parents, teachers, peers, or at work if we want to follow the path of least resistance. We say, "Yeah, it is nice to see you too…" (insert fake smile here) while our inner voice says, "Get me out of here!" It does not feel good to fake smile or hide our emotions. Be real and be genuine, and your best smile will always shine through.

Besides, faking a smile is not very effective because you can never hide your emotions from anyone that spends time with you or is present with you. If my kids are upset, all I have to do is be around them to know. If my wife is not happy with something my kids or I did, it is pretty easy to know when Mom is not happy. :) If you simply talk with someone or ask them how they are feeling, you can very quickly tell if they are feeling good, bad, upset, or happy. So if you need to fake a smile, do what you have to do! If something happens or someone says something that takes away our smile, be aware of it; don't ignore it. And more importantly, remind yourself to let it go and not give the power of your feelings and your meanings over to external opinions and external circumstances. We control how we feel unless we give that power away to someone or something outside of us. We should never let anyone or anything take our smile away.

You can't make me smile!

Overbite Smile

I'd like to share with you the story of my patient and friend, Linda. She really helped me to understand the power of smiling in an entirely different way. Linda is in her early thirties, and she is so over-the-top happy. I had to know how she does it, so I asked, "Linda, every time I see you, you have such a great smile, have you always been this way?"

"Well thank you! Yes, I have done this for most of my life. I started when I was a teenager. I had a pretty extreme overbite, and I didn't like how I looked. I realized that when I looked in the mirror and smiled, it made my overbite less noticeable and I started smiling all the time!" She was grinning and nodding her head delightfully yet emphatically to articulate her point.

"So, do you feel you are happier because of this?" I asked.

"Absolutely. I have problems like everyone else, and when the you-know-what hits the fan, I just put on my smile and get through it!" Linda is absolutely unflappable.

She continues, "Yeah, I had a guy-friend I used to hang out with, and he would tell me 'Linda, you always seem so happy, I just like being around you because it makes me feel good!' He may have thought that he was the reason I smiled so much—and he wasn't—but I didn't burst his bubble." She laughed. "And my girlfriend was telling me she couldn't believe how I seemed joyful when I had so much drama in my life. I needed a major surgery recently, and yet I still keep a positive outlook on things. I pretty much smile through the good and the bad, and it has made a huge difference in my life!"

We love when Linda comes into the office, and she certainly makes my staff and me smile. As they say, everyone can make the room smile. Some do it when they arrive, and some do it because they leave. Genuine smiles are contagious! We are drawn to people that smile. Smiling is the most attractive thing we do to our face, as it literally *attracts* other people to us. Smiling also brings us compliments, and that makes us feel good about ourselves! So why not smile more? What have you got to lose? Nothing at all!

Do you surround yourself with things that make you smile?

Do You Have Abundance In Your Smile?

Yes, no, maybe? Okay, isn't it a shame how people tend to focus on the negative, even though they are surrounded by positive circumstances? If you do have abundance in your smile, way to go! If you don't, then why not? Take a moment to consider the following: we all know people that smile no matter what happens to them, don't we? Remember Linda, with the overbite smile? These are the types of people we love to be around. Are you one of these people? If you are grateful for your abundance, then your smile is much easier to share. We can be like the kid who has it all, but is so upset because he dropped his ice cream on the floor, or we can realize that we have a lot to smile about in our lives!

If you look, it isn't hard to find the abundance in life that will make you smile. But, what about the person that goes to work and hates their job? Their manager says to them in a sing-song voice, "Okay, everyone smile for the customer please!" For the person that resents their work and feels overwhelmed by challenges and struggles at home, just telling them to smile isn't going to work. He or she may be facing overdue bills, or they are suffering an illness that is wearing them out emotionally, physically, and financially. Instead of making this person smile, we can make them feel angry! What is the solution for this smile dilemma? If that is you, don't give up! Don't play the victim. Believe in yourself and just lighten up! See the bigger picture, start investing in yourself and the people around you, you will get out of the rut and find your smile. Resentment can be turned into pride, and you can start to increase your influence in other's lives while making a significant impact in your world.

So if you are in a management or leadership position, here are some quick tips on how to make almost anyone smile. I included two lists below, one that is tame and docile, for those who may be more nerdy or a bookworm like me, and one for those who are really ready to be outrageous and get their smile on. :-) Have faith in the people that you work with, and I promise you these steps will bring out their smiles. Here's a tip, when leaders love people more than their position, their position is strengthened, and soon so are their people. So let's get to smiling. :) No matter how engaging your personality may be or how effective you are, you will not advance far if you cannot do work through others.

Here are the areas where you can improve being a smile influencer. Take the necessary steps to smile yourself and increase your impact on the lives of those around you. The greater your influence, the greater your opportunity for personal and organizational success. The office (and family) that smiles together, stays together.

The Docile Smile List:

1. Smile yourself and increase the impact in the lives of those around you! Do not just ask others to smile. This never works. This was the mistake I made, and I apologize to those that suffered through my learning curve.

2. Find something fun or funny about what your team does. It is okay to be a clown when you are helping others smile. Your team may think you are a clown anyway, they just haven't told you. :)

3. Employee of the week or month is a powerful way to reinforce smiles. Recognize someone for a job well done, it always means more when it comes from the heart and puts a smile on their face.

4.   Lighten up and have fun. Let your team know you enjoy them.

5.   Speak to staff individually to ask them what you can do to get the team smiling more. Use the language, "I need your help," or "How can we get our team smiling and having more fun?" **Listen, listen, listen** to what they tell you!

6.   Play games or be playful in the office. Hide and go seek or tag. Twister is not so practical. :)

7.   Social gatherings, breakfast, or lunch with the office is great for letting the team blow off steam and alleviate friction that builds up.

Outrageous Smile List:

1.   Fall down on the floor in front of your team (don't hurt yourself!). It works for America's Funniest Home Videos. :)

2.   Instead of walking, just dance when you are moving from place to place! Don't do this on the tabletops. :)

3.   Take an unflattering picture of yourself and share it with others just to get them to smile. Chin down or face down really brings out the best in us!

4.   If you have slow-motion video mode on your phone or camera, take a video of you or your friend sticking out their tongue and making the "Thhhhpppppttttt!!" raspberry sound. This is always a winner.

5.   Whoopee cushion.

6.   Do a video conference with someone while your camera is upside down.

7.   Raise your hands up in the air and put a big smile on your face when you greet people.

8.   On Throwback Thursday, post a baby picture of yourself in your diapers. Adorable!

These tips are easy to do, fun, and help build amazing rapport amongst your team. Coming up next are fun questions for *you*! You should probably brush your teeth and use mouthwash before you start because your smile will be getting a lot of use. :) Let's get started on creating abundance in your smile! The ability to smile at anything in life creates wealth beyond measure.

Smiling Makes Good Karma

Did you pick up any good tips in the Smile Lists? Start practicing alone or with your family and friends, because our smiles connect us to others and are absolutely good for our karma! And wouldn't you know it, I found a research study that backs this up! U.C. Berkeley[5] actually performed a study demonstrating the long-term effects of smiling. They showed that when you smile more, you are more likely to be married and have a higher level of general well-being. That is what I call good karma. :) They rated the smiling habits of female students in their yearbook photos aged twenty or twenty-one, putting them into one of three categories: No smile, genuine smile, or fake smile. These women were later contacted up to thirty years later, and information was gathered on their personal, family, and work life. The overall results showed that women who demonstrated a "positive emotional expression," or a more genuine smile in their yearbook photos, were much more likely to be married and have a higher level of general wellbeing. Wow! It is truly powerful to see science prove that our facial expressions can forecast the future. Yearbooks have traditionally named students "Most Likely to Succeed" and "Best Looking." Maybe now they will pick "Who Is Most Likely to Remain in a Long-Term Relationship and Have a Higher Sense of Wellbeing!"

If this yearbook smile study is not enough for you, Depauw University[6] made a similar investigation, this time to see how smile intensity predicts divorce later in life. They looked at a variety of home photos from 655 college grads. They found that when studying family photos, those with fewer or weaker smiles had a higher rate of divorce. Very interesting trend! So next time you take a picture, you better SMILE! Your life, happiness, and marriage depend on it! And, if you are dating someone that might be the keeper you've been looking for, aren't you curious as to whether your partner was smiling in their yearbook or home pictures? Every chance we get to smile is an opportunity well worth taking!

To my wife Irene, the woman of my dreams: This is my "We are going to be married forever" high school yearbook smile.

Smile Stronger, Live Longer

Smiling reduces our rate of divorce and makes us happier, but can it actually make us live longer? Yes, it does that too. In 2009, Wayne State University[7] looked at 230 pictures from the 1952 register for major league baseball players. Similar categories were used: no smile, fake smile, or genuine smile. Big surprise, those with genuine smiles in their pictures lived to almost eighty, while the fake smilers tended to pass at seventy-five. The non-smilers passed at about seventy-three. Twenty smiles a day keeps the plastic surgeon *and* doctor away! And whatever the mechanism is, if smiling has been shown to improve wellbeing, increase the likelihood of staying married, decrease the likelihood of divorce, and increase longevity, then I think we have found something worth doing! Maybe the surgeon general needs to issue warning labels for non-smiling faces. **WARNING: Failure to smile may result in a reduction in your life, marriage, and happiness.**

The more we smile, the longer we live.

What Stimulates Your Smile?

Smile Shocks

Did you know that smiling and laughing are programmed into our brain? I love this story; it is going blow your mind on how this works! Dr. Itzahk Fried is a neurosurgery professor at UCLA, and what he found is literally shocking in every sense of the word.[8] Dr. Fried's team delivered electricity to a woman's brain to stimulate smiling and laughing! It sounds like a taser that makes you laugh! As the story goes, the test subject was instructed to perform unrelated tasks, such as reading, counting, or moving her hands and feet. When they delivered very small amounts of electricity to the front of her brain, she consistently demonstrated a smile. At higher currents, a "robust and contagious laughter" was induced, and the higher the current, the longer the duration and intensity of the laughter. This laughter was accompanied by a sensation of mirth and merriment, and when the current got high enough, she would stop performing all other activities while laughing. When the laughter was stimulated with electric shocks, she associated whatever she was doing at the time with being "funny." Stand-up comics around the world are dying to learn about this technology! :)

If the test subject was reading about a horse and received the stimulation, she thought the horse was funny. If she was talking to people in the room during stimulation, she thought the people were funny. If you let this sink in, the implications are astonishing. Our brain is like a computer, and brain cells (neurons) work using electricity and chemicals (neurotransmitters is the fancy word for these chemicals in our brain). This electrical and chemical stimulation creates "shocks" in our brain all the time, and we use these shocks to control our body to move, sing, read, laugh, eat, play, or sleep. Just like this young lady, we can give ourselves "Smile Shocks" and stimulate our own brain to feel however we want to feel. We can choose what we find to be funny or not funny. And we can rehearse and strengthen the behavior patterns and neural networks that we choose with these brain shocks. Kind of creepy, and the good news is that you don't need to hook batteries up to your head to make this happen. Just practice your smile and give your brain a smiling power surge!

Basic neurophysiology tells us that stimulating (or shocking) the brain is how we get better at a musical instrument, sport, language, or any discipline for that matter. By constantly stimulating a specific area of our brain, we consistently improve that behavior. It is like building a muscle. The more you stimulate it, the more that area develops. Doesn't it feel good to be stimulated? So let's make sure we stimulate ourselves (shock our brain) in behaviors that are favorable and serve us. This strategy also works when you stimulate and reinforce behaviors relating to anger, sadness, depression, and rage. And, all of our brain stimulation ultimately comes from within. So here is the question: Are you controlling what stimulates your brain? Or, are you letting other people or external factors shock your brain and control what stimulates your behaviors? Who is minding your mind? If you don't mind your mind, someone else will start controlling it. Frankenstein had the bolts on the sides of his neck just in case his brain needed a jumpstart. Just think of people in the same way, and sometimes they need a "smile shock" to get their smile going. Always keep your jumper cables handy!

We can Jumpstart a Smile in Anyone!

The Evidence Is In!

Now you can understand why this is so important to me. :) The evidence is clear that smiling and creating positive meaning in your life will make you happier, reduce your stress, and help you live longer. This supports our Smile Hypothesis we stated at the beginning of the chapter:

Proactive, genuine smiling will increase happiness, the quality of relationships, health, longevity, and emotional resilience.

On the other hand, lack of smiling correlates to feelings of sadness, depression, and a shorter life span. This is so important, we have created a simple five step fun process that everyone can follow to enhance their smile. Isn't it fun to learn about the magic in life? Now, if you liked chapter two, I promise that you will absolutely ADORE chapter three! Check out our "Five-Step Smile Blossom" below, and we will see you in chapter three to get started on blossoming your smile!

DOCTOR'S ORDERS:

1. Practice the Facial Feedback Hypothesis by changing your facial expression. Remember: Face = Feelings.

2. Share with others how the research tells us to SMILE.

3. Help your smile muscles win the battle of the Brow - Don't give in to the frown muscles!

4. Guard yourself from the self-conscious, frosty, or fake smiles that will bring you down.

5. Control your "Smile Shocks," otherwise you may let external influences stimulate your behaviors.

6. Smile stronger and live longer; the easiest way to age more gracefully (Baseball Card Study).

SMILE REFLECTIONS:

- What are you thankful or grateful for in your life?

- Are there things in your life that are bringing your smile down?

- Can you use your smile to turn around any negative situations you come across?

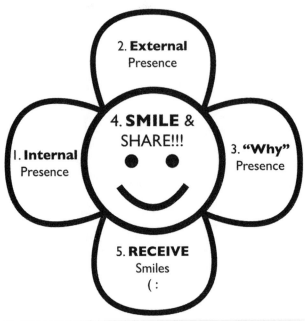

The Smile Blossom—Five Easy Steps to Improving Anyone's Smile

"Now hurry up and finish your reading, otherwise you'll go straight to your room when your father gets home."

chapter three

FACE
PRESENCE

"Being present is the *most control* we will ever have over our lives. Presence is necessary for a genuine smile." :) Dr. Rich

"We convince by our presence." — Walt Whitman

This is the chapter that my wife Irene thinks is the coolest. :) It will focus on being more present in the moment, which will enhance your life and bring out your best smile. Being present can bring serenity and peace, and it is available to us at any time. Can you remember a time that you have been completely tranquil and at peace in the moment? Chapter three will assist you in creating more of these moments which will certainly bring out your smile.

When combining presence with the research and information revealed in chapter two, you now have the firepower to win any smile debate with even the frowniest of doubters out there. Tell them to bring it on! Your smile shows your presence, and smiling is one of the most powerful and natural facial expressions you will ever create! This is why the real secret weapon to settle any smile-spat is...by actually using your SMILE! Silence the crankiest of smile critics with the power of your smile. When smile doubters see how happy your smile makes you, there is nothing left to say. There is great power in communicating without words. When you try to reason and debate with words and logic, it never compares with the feeling we all get when our face expresses a sincere and genuine smile.

Presence = Peacefulness, Stimulating, and Fun

It is so natural for us to smile. We often stop or censor ourselves because of cultural norms. We are constantly being told what to do and to, "Get Serious!" Anyone who watches kids knows how easy it is to get them laughing and smiling, and good luck getting them to quiet down once they really get giggling! As a kid myself I often got into trouble for laughing when I shouldn't. I'll bet this has happened to you at sometime in your life. And you know how hard it is to stop laughing when something is really funny! Yet as we grow, we are told over and over again to settle down, get control of ourselves, and that we need to be more serious about things. Has that ever happened to you? Well, we have heard this so many times, that many people have blunted or stunted their ability to smile freely, leaving them unable to truly be present with their smile when they need to. Let's set the foundation for creating a genuine smile with our Five Step Smile Process! Here it is again in our Smile Blossom diagram:

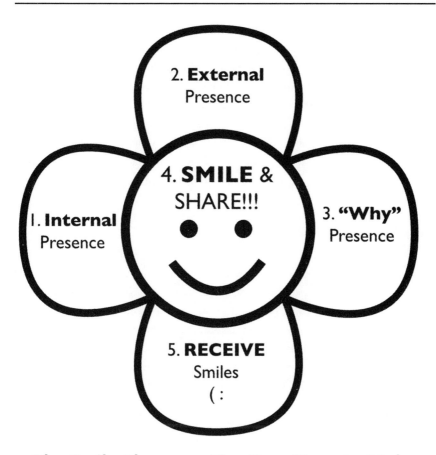

The Smile Blossom - Five Easy Steps to Make Anyone's Smile Bloom

Step 1: **Be present internally. Develop the presence of your "Smile Bud." Listen to and focus on understanding your body and yourself.**

Step 2: Be present externally. Unfold your petals, expand your presence and focus, and be open to your environment and those people around you.

Step 3: Be present with your "why." Pollinate your world with empowering meaning.

Step 4: SMILE and have fun with it! Enjoy your flowering beauty and create a bouquet of smiles by helping friends and family to smile with you.

Step 5: Receive and complete the cycle of happiness. Validate and encourage others to grow their smile blossoms, smile bouquets, and happiness.

The Five Step Smile Process in Detail

So let's get started on improving the impact of your smile! How do we know if we are getting the most from the power of our smile? Is it possible we are missing a few key smile distinctions that cost us our most important relationships or the competitive edge at work? *The Smile Prescription* is dedicated to enhancing and creating the absolute best smile for you and those around you! Can you imagine promoting genuine and healthful smiles, while creating happiness and abundance? We must have the courage to follow along and the willingness to change if we need to grow. The value here is limitless, so let the smiles shine through!

Step One: Be Present Internally

People ask me all the time, "What is presence?" So let me explain that to you now. Presence is simply the focus of our attention. When I am in surgery, I am focused in the moment, on my patient, without distractions so that I do the best job I can and do not hurt anyone. Believe it or not, we have this same presence when we put a smile on our face. Whenever you have a genuine smile, you are being present with something that you like and are happy about, without distractions.

We are said "to be present" when we engage in the here and now. This is very well described in Eckhart Tolle's classic book *The Power of Now,* and I highly recommend that you read (or reread) it. Tolle describes how nothing exists except for the present. The past is gone forever, never to return, and the future hasn't happened yet. All we have is the "now" and to be present. The rest is in our mind and imagination. Do you ever find that people aren't present in life or that they lack focus? Everyone is present with something in life and does focus. The question is, what are they being present with and where is their focus? Is their attention on the cell phone, at work, with bills, worrying or frustrating, or trying to focus on everything all at the same time? Many people can focus on distractions and ignore all of the ingredients for a happy life right in front of them. Being present with our distractions is never as fulfilling as being present with what is most important to us, and this distracts us from our smile.

Genuine presence is a magnificent experience, because it is one of the greatest gifts you will give or receive. Yet are most people really present with others, even when they are having a direct conversation with them? Not if you see them checking their cell phone, or their eyes are scanning the room while talking with someone right in front of them. And what about being present with the road and traffic when they are driving? Our lives depend on being present behind the wheel. This chapter dives into the most calming, peaceful, and tranquil practice of being truly present. I have found that the key to being present is being aware of what our focus is, and then moving beyond the inevitable distractions. Guess what? Most of these distractions come from the voices and dialogue going on in our head! It is amazing to see the things we allow in our consciousness. It brings to mind the morning I went to breakfast at my sons' school.

Dressed and ready for success!

Dropping the Kids Off at School

I was dropping my two boys, Xavier and Domenic, off at school. Domenic is nine, and he is at a stage where he can be very sweet and considerate! He loves to hold my hand as we walk to class. Xavier is the epitome of cool at the age of seven, and he doesn't want to hold hands as much. As we are walking into school, Xavier says, "I'm hungry!" Even though I knew he had already eaten breakfast at home, I dropped him off at the cafeteria and walk Domenic to his class.

After getting Domenic situated, I doubled back to the cafeteria to sit with Xavier. There are kids everywhere, bouncing in from the bus, standing in line for food, or sitting at the tables eating. Everyone is hanging out, waking up, or joking with their friends. It was like the nature channel where I could watch these kids in their native environment and I was invisible as they were catching up with each other, sharing their big smiling faces.

I follow Xavier from the food line to the table, and thankfully he picks a seat where I can sit with him. There are some parents peppered around the cafeteria, and some of them are smiling and interacting with their kids. The rest have on their pre-coffee tired-looking faces and are either looking into their phones, tying their kid's shoelaces, or carrying book bags to class. A few are glancing toward the clock, waiting for the bell to ring so they can leave.

A young girl named Mandy with big, curly hair walks up and sits across from Xavier. "This is the second breakfast I've been to," she says slowly, with a sweet and innocent smile on her face. The boy next to her is more serious as he looks up, "I've been to breakfast seventeen times this year." His face is solemn, and that is the end of their conversation. Mandy gives an adorable and simple smile, and says it again to herself, "Two times I've been to breakfast here." She spoons more cereal into her mouth. I had to stop myself from laughing out loud, the moment was so pure and genuine.

Xavier starts up a conversation with Sebastian who is sitting next to him. He asks with a smile, "Sebastian, would you rather have a duck or a chicken?"

Sebastian starts smiling too, thinking about how fun this chicken-challenge is. After a brief pause of smiling contemplation, he says, "A chicken!" His smile grows even wider, like he is really going to get one!

Really?!? I can't let that go, I have to know. "Sebastian, why do you want a chicken?" His big smile returns, and he says, "Um, well, Thanksgiving is coming up, and this way we can have a nice fried chicken for dinner!" Okay, that makes sense—very practical, very simple, and certainly smile-worthy.

I look around at the adults in the cafeteria, no doubt with a lot on their minds. Very few of them appear to be present in the moment and smiling. The kids are talking to one another, and smiling a lot more than the adults. They are present with the immediate world right in front of them. The kids are thinking simpler thoughts, and smiling more. The adults who seem to be scattered and unfocused tend to smile less.

The more simply we think and the more present we are, the more we smile. If the adults were able to clear their minds, enjoy the simple matters, and be more present in the moment, would they smile more? Would the world be a happier place if we all took on the chicken challenge more often? I think so, what do you think?

Do you ever observe children as they play?

Observe Kids and Simplify Your Thoughts

Have you ever noticed how much fun it is to observe children as they play? Watch what they pay attention to, what they say, how they act, and what they are present with. Now, how would you feel if you said what they say and do EXACTLY what they do? The only way to really know is to do it. :) You probably will look foolish doing this, so please don't hold back if you desire to really experience what they are feeling! :) Years ago, I started observing and writing down how children and people play when they are having fun, and it has changed my life. We can suffer from analysis paralysis all too easily, and being playfully present is the absolute opposite of this. Children can be our best coaches for presence and smiling. Create your own story of presence, play, and smiling. When we say, "Out of the mouths of babes..." that is all about how kids seem so intelligent. Their secret is that they are just very present in the moment.

"To get back one's youth one has merely to repeat one's follies."— Oscar Wilde

What are some simple thoughts that you like to think? How does it feel to let yourself focus on the little things in life without letting the distractions come in?

83

Your inner critic may think that you look or sound silly during this exercise but go ahead and tell them to give you a break. Encourage your inner dialogue to not be so overbearing or over-boring. Cut yourself some slack! You will need to ignore those voices for a few moments, and have some fun.

"Make me one with everything."

Being present comes in many forms.

Being Present, Prayer, and Meditation

Meditation Improves Your Health

I will use the terms presence, prayer, and meditation interchangeably through this chapter as they all share similar qualities: quiet time, peacefulness, reflection, relaxation, restoration, soulfulness, and spirituality. It makes you feel peaceful just thinking about those words. :) You don't have to be religious to benefit from what we are talking about here, though it is important to recognize that religion is a fundamental part of our world. If you think about it, religion touches almost every aspect of our lives, and there is evidence to show that religious involvement is correlated with better mental health with regard to depression, substance abuse, and suicide.[1] And it doesn't hurt your smile either! :) So whether or not you are religious or spiritual, we are going to tap into the power of spirituality on a basic level so you can see and feel how that impacts your smile.

Just take some chances to break through your comfort zone by trying it for yourself! I always feel a sense of calm and peacefulness when I quiet my mind. Have you felt this yet? For many years research has demonstrated that meditation and being present improves anxiety, depression, and pain.[2] This was recently published again in JAMA, the *Journal of the American Medical Association* (or as my kids call it, the PaJAMA magazine). This is better information than what you might read in People magazine, Vogue, or Men's Health! Brilliant researchers across the country and all over the world have published that even substance abuse and eating disorders can be improved with meditation and practices that quiet the mind.[3-5] Sounds like we are on to something here…

I like to think about meditation and being present like noise cancelling technology for your headphones. Noise cancelling blocks out distracting sounds so you can focus on the music you are listening to. Have you ever tried on a pair? Listening through regular headphones is great, but when you use noise cancelling technology, you can hear things much more clearly than before, and after you have tried them, it is hard to go back to regular headphones! Being present and meditating function in the same way by cancelling out the external noises in your world so you can focus on the "music" of your life experience. You will definitely be impressed when you try this "higher fidelity" experience out. Quiet your mind and see for yourself!

Here is something fun to do: One of my favorite ways to be present is to just smile and stare blankly into the distance. I call it the "Blank-Stare Smile" or the "Space-Out Smile." If you do this long enough, people will look at you and wonder if you've lost your mind! The answer is no, actually you have found your mind and are in control of it. When you are in control of your mind, you have the ability to slow or stop the thoughts coming through your head. We don't have to automatically fall into default thoughts about problems, challenges, bills, heartaches, or relationship upsets. When I do the blank-stare smile, I am being totally present with my smile, with feeling good, and it feels glorious! Yet most people are uncomfortable doing this.

When we are smiling big and laughing, we have rediscovered our minds. I invite you to smile and stare blankly into the distance, either in a room alone or in front of a mirror. You need to trust me, I'm the Smile Doctor! I took the Hippocratic Oath, I care about you, and these are Doctor's Orders. :) Make no mistake, this is a very silly practice. That is okay, there are many, many things we do in life that are silly, and the blank-stare smile will fit right in. This is the face we make when we are in a total state of bliss, feeling absolute joy and ecstasy. You take a bite of your favorite food, and it tastes so good, you stare blankly into the distance, and you let out a deep breath while saying, "Whoa" or "Wow!" You travel on vacation, you look out over the Grand Canyon, Niagara Falls, or other landmark, and you smile with the blank stare on your face at what is in front of you. We also look around to see if anyone else is being present with this exceptional moment. It is special when we are present with one another together. We love to share, and that is why it is so important to share our smile. The blank-stare smile is so important because it allows you to totally connect with yourself, in total concentration, like a laser beam, being completely internal. You are able to connect with everything in your being, and this has everything to do with being alive and being present.

I confess, this is a bit of a detour from *The Smile Prescription*, but am I really asking you to do something totally inane and pointless? Follow along with me, and consider the story of Thich Nhat Hanh. He is a Buddhist monk who has written many books on meditation and quieting the mind. He tells a story about a dear friend he loves to visit with. Their visits are not what you would expect. He greets his friend, and they share no words. They prepare and drink tea together, and there is no verbal exchange. They are simply experiencing each other's presence. After drinking the tea, Thich Nhat Hanh would leave and be on his way. He describes his friend as a treasure because these visits help him to be grounded by being centered in a world filled with distractions. The blank-stare smile is like the "tea without words" experience, because there are no words or running dialogue when you sit and are present with your smile. There is just your mind, your body, and your smile, and they are existing together, experiencing one another, observing, receiving, and not transmitting with words. :)

You should do this alone to stay focused. Though, it is really fun to use the blank-stare smile to make other people smile. When they see me and ask, "What are you doing?!?" I tell them, "I'm turning off all the racket in my brain!" This is a type of meditation that helps you to shut out the constant barrage we all face from stress, news of catastrophes, crime, fear, and panic. It feels good to get a break from this negativity in our world! It is so easy for me to be playful with the blank-stare smile and share my joy and bliss. When people ask what you are doing, tell them the truth, "I am playing with my smile and experiencing euphoria! It feels good, and I'm trying to get you to smile too!" Being present and centered will absolutely help you to smile more easily. It's okay to be selfish with this feeling, and hold onto it because it allows you to see who you really are inside when you aren't distracted by what is going on around you. The blank-stare smile is an investment in yourself. It feels good, and we need this feeling to balance out the tension and anxiety we invite into our lives. The funniest thing about the blank-stare smile is that it is for you and no one else, yet it provokes a response from people when you do it around them.

I love the blank-stare smile because it is peaceful and it quiets the mind, even if it is a little foolish :) When you quiet the mind, researchers (that you could read about in JAMA) have demonstrated that well-being and quality of life improve.[6, 7] Many people agree with this intuitively, yet how many take the time to pray or quiet the mind? Whether or not you pray, prayer is a way to connect with yourself internally. For those of you who do not pray, prayer is still a form of meditation. Improving the quality of our life requires a conscious decision to do so. Enhancing your ability to be present is like any other skill, talent, or ability you cultivate. The more you do it, the better you get. So let's give ourselves a workout in being present! Many people know this practice is beneficial, though they don't do it. We know that going to the gym or exercising consistently will strengthen and tone our body. Yet sometimes we still do not make the time to exercise. If you make the time to meditate or quiet your mind, you will strengthen your will and learn to be at peace with your life. Don't we all benefit from taking a break from our stress? If you are unable to be present in the moment, it will hinder your ability to smile. And when you are present in the moment, you will immediately feel how much easier it is to smile when you can purposely direct your focus. Pretty cool stuff!

Jerry Seinfeld tells the story about how his show rose to fame. I highly recommend you watch this on YouTube, it was very insightful! Seinfeld is the Michael Jordan of comedy, (or is Michael Jordan the Seinfeld of the NBA?) and he certainly knows how to make people smile. Jerry Seinfeld speaks openly about how he is a regular practitioner of transcendental meditation. Transcendental meditation calms the mind using a chant, sound, or mantra for ten to twenty minutes, twice daily. Seinfeld says he would clear his mind using this practice and that it was necessary for fueling his creativity, which of course led to many millions of smiles.

I also like to think of clearing the mind like using an Etch-a-Sketch. You can't make a new drawing or masterpiece if your screen is full of other drawings. To do your best work, you must have the cleanest canvas you can find or create. Or, think of quieting the mind like closing all of the apps on your smartphone, tablet, or computer. When we have dozens of applications open at the same time, your phone/tablet/computer runs slower, and can even crash. The apps we usually have open in our mind are one or more of the four F's: family, finances, fitness, and friends. Close all of these apps with your blank-stare smile or meditation, and now your mind-device works better and the information flows faster. We think much more slowly when we are tired or have too many things on our mind. It often goes under our radar when our brain is overburdened and overworked, and we don't realize we are functioning in slow-motion. You feel it right away when you quiet your mind how much clearer and faster your thinking is. So clear that screen, close those apps, close your eyes, and shake up that smile! Your smiling mind is the coolest high-tech gadget that has ever been made, better than any phone, tablet, or computer. :) Our brain is a biological computer that has amazing processing speed, great memory capacity, can speak many languages, is infinitely upgradable, and it is portable and rechargeable! Now that is a cool gadget!

Are You Ready to Improve Your Presence?

Did you snap out of your blank-stare smile yet? I have only had a few complaints about people getting stuck in that smile, though I am pretty sure it is a temporary problem... In addition to tons of research supporting the positive benefits of being present and meditating, it has now been demonstrated how meditation physically changes our brain.[8] Pretty creepy! A study from Harvard showed that seventeen test subjects undergoing an eight-week mindfulness training, increased their gray matter in specific areas of the brain.[9]

We talked about this with our smile shocks. Whenever we stimulate the body, the body responds and changes. Stimulating muscles causes them to grow. Stimulating bone with weight bearing exercises increases bone density. Stimulating the brain will also cause it to change. When the areas of the brain for meditation are stimulated, they respond and develop so that the brain physically changes. Any behavior that is repeated and reinforced becomes easier and more effective with time because our brain forms new neural connections and rewires based on our behavior patterns. There are also studies that show how hand coordination, musical ability, geographical memory, grammar ability and more have all been shown to demonstrate changes in the physical structure of our brain.[10] When I stimulate my brain with meditation, I like to focus on my breathing, feel my feet as I am meditating while walking, or listen to the numerous sounds in my environment. This feels so good, it is guaranteed to bring a smile to your face!

One more time, think of your mind like an Etch-a-Sketch inside your head, where you can redesign the pattern each time if you choose to draw over the same area! The only difference is if you shake your head up too much it won't wipe everything out :) Even when we do clear our mind, we can always find behavior and thought patterns again because they are much more deeply ingrained than what we realize. This ability to rewire our brain is profoundly important. I can not think of a greater art form available to humankind beyond sculpting and shaping our brain and our consciousness. Think about the masterpieces we all create as we build and grow our character and personalities. Picasso could never create something as profound as the artistry of the billions of neural pathways in our brain that make up our own individuality. Our personality and our identity are made up of the artistry, noise, and quietness we put in our mind. Too many people think they are stuck with their behaviors, and nothing could be further from the truth. Our brains are always "under construction," never finished, always improving, and always responding to what we feed our mind and what we expose ourselves to.

"Think about the masterpieces we all create as we build and grow our character and personality. The artistry, graffiti, noise, and quiet of our mind becomes our personality and our identity." — Dr. Rich

Now wait a minute! If you start rewiring and reprogramming your brain, are you going to delete some important files or crash the hard drive in your head?!? Who can you call for tech support if your brain is on the fritz? Don't worry, you must repeat these behaviors of change if you desire to change the wiring of your brain. Our thoughts can be like graffiti. Thoughts are fickle, can come and go, and can easily be covered. Though the graffiti of our brain is harder to remove when it is reinforced over and over again. Once you have made those physical changes in your brain that come from repetitive behaviors, it is easier to perform these new behaviors and your skill becomes better! And, it is more difficult to revert to previous behaviors once you have physically changed your brain with your newly reinforced behavior patterns. Said more simply, put yourself out there and fake it till you make it! Your brain will rewire to support your new behaviors. Redesigning your brain may sound like hard work, but it is really fun when you put a smile on your face. :) More practice and more effort makes new behaviors stronger! Yes, it can take many days to form a new habit, and there is great power in repetition. We can shorten this learning curve when we increase our intensity, energy, and smiling, with these new behaviors. Getting your energy or adrenaline higher and your smile bigger with new behaviors will help you to form habits more quickly. And all of this brain and behavior modification starts with being present.

"Sculpting and reshaping our consciousness is the highest form of human artistry. The greatest tools to prepare the canvas of our mind are presence, meditation, and prayer." — Dr. Rich

Are you clearing the canvas of your mind with your presence, or are you letting the distractions in life clutter your masterpiece?

Practicing Presence with Kids

My boys are normal seven and nine year olds, and they fight with each other, just like I fought with my brother when I was younger—good times bro! Their behavior can be so CRAZY that sometimes they have a hard time settling down (I wonder where they get this from :)

90

**Sure I fought with my brothers when I was younger,
just not in front of the camera.**

I decided we should practice being quiet and present for five minutes. No problem, that is a short enough time for kids to practice, right? I have meditation chimes, I will let the peaceful sound vibrations ring to give them something to focus on. There is no doubt that we are well on our way to full emotional control for high energy kids that are unruly before bedtime. "Okay, let's sit down very gently like frogs on a lily pad. If you shake or move too much, you will fall in the water!" I demonstrate. "Okay, now we are going to calm ourselves down. Is it better that we control our tiger, or that our tiger controls us?" (We use the word "tiger" to describe our emotions that can sometimes control us, as demonstrated in *The Life of Pi*). The boys respond in unison, "We control our tiger."

"Are you sure?!" I reaffirm. "Yes!" they yell back with certainty. Okay, at least it sounds like they are on board. We sit and I gently sound the chimes. The boys are quiet, and all looks well until five seconds into our session when they start to peek at each other and begin with the tiny tee-hee snickering. I focus on them to get their attention and try to use my presence and energy to infuse calm into the room. This does not work. In fact, they escalate into giggles. I sound the chimes again, and instead of helping them focus, it throws them over into outright laughter. I tried my blank-stare smile, and I imagined myself being Thich Nhat Hanh having tea without words. All to no avail, as my kids now are the ones in control. What

91

happened to the quiet? Did we make any progress? My wife yells from downstairs, "Boys, settle down, it is time for bed!!" How did a session on presence and quietude end with Mom yelling at all of us?

I fearlessly jump in to wrestle back the control I never really had. "Okay guys, why don't you look away from each other, you need to learn to quiet yourselves down. This is important!" They are separated by five feet and are back-to-back, but they keep giggling because they can still hear each other. "Okay, that is enough." My voice breaks, and I can't continue talking because it is all so funny I start laughing too. And then the boys REALLY start laughing because Dad is laughing now. AAAGGHHHH! I am doing my best to reshape the gray matter in their heads, though their existing gray matter for laughing and rowdiness is proving to be stronger than my gray matter for quietness and calm! At the end of the session, we were smiling and laughing, everyone was exhausted, and it did not take them long to get to sleep that night. That made Mom smile too! Score one for Dad :)

We have had much more success on subsequent sessions. And lets face it, raising kids really requires a lifetime of prayer, meditation, calming strategies, and smiling and laughing to cope and get through, for both the kids AND the parents. We are just getting started. I confess, it is not always easy to meditate. It is like everything else, you get out of it what you put into it. Or, if you are able to let go of your frustrations, worries, fears, anxieties, and stress, then you will get out of it what you do not put into it, if that makes sense. With practice, I promise it will all come together. It is fun and worth the effort. Don't let meditation melt-downs or failures discourage you. Have faith in the process and keep smiling as you focus on being present in the moment!

Presence and Tranquility Made Simple

I invite you to think about how all the channels of our body are open for the free movement of creativity and spirituality when we allow ourselves to be present and smile. It is like flipping the light-switch on in the room. Now you can see everything in front of you, where it was totally dark before. If being present is so important to our smile and to rewiring our brain, what are the keys to quieting the mind and enhancing your thinking and creativity? Follow these three steps for best results:

1. **Have faith** that quieting the mind, meditation, or being present works. You must BELIEVE.

2. **Block your schedule** at a specific time for this activity to avoid distractions. Give yourself at least ten minutes a day.

3. **Be patient and flexible**. Persist until it works for you. Quitting is not an option! :)

Drama, tears, love, and smiles; isn't the craziness in all families picture perfect?

First of all, faith in the process is imperative. We know the sun will rise and set, and the seasons will come to pass. We are certain that at some point, we will hunger for our next meal. Allow yourself to know and have faith that calming the mind will work for you as it has worked for billions of people. Regardless of what you personally believe in, faith is an important part of our world. In the United States, a 2012 Gallup poll showed that almost 4 out of 5 people identify a religious preference. Religious practices all have some form of prayer, quietude, or meditation. I am not here to tell you what to believe spiritually, though I am going to encourage you to practice something that allows you to calm your mind and explore. What do you have to lose? I believe you will be amazed and inspired by attending a place of worship, regardless of the denomination, to experience and explore spirituality and incorporate this into your life in whatever form you are able.

Faith can be hard for some people to have because they never allow themselves to strongly believe in anything. Being open to your faith will certainly lift up your smile. :) A life without faith is a life full of doubt. No one ever lived their best life doubting everything. What do you believe in? Believe in something, even if it is yourself you are believing in. Consider that when you do have faith, it makes you smile. You believe. You know what will come. It makes you happy. And when you lose your faith, it will wipe the smile right off of your face. How you use (or don't use) your faith will profoundly impact your ability to smile and create happiness in your life. I pray every night with my family, and this practicing of our presence is something that brings us closer together and absolutely helps us to smile more.

Are you blocking time to be present?

So are you now able to sing along with the immortal words of the Monkees, "I'm a Believer!" I'm not asking you to join a smile church, but using your faith is a fun way to practice presence and your smile. Beyond having faith and believing in your presence, the real key to making this work is blocking your schedule and setting time aside to be present. I know, I know, everyone is busy and no one has time. What, are you in jail or something? If you say you have no control over your schedule, you actually are incarcerated, even if it is by your own choice. If you are being held captive in an abusive situation, please do whatever you can to escape! And if you actually are in a prison, you should have time to block your schedule to quiet the mind.

Whatever your circumstance is, just block your schedule and tell everyone that you have an unbreakable appointment with a VIP. Because you are a VIP! We all know a plant will not grow unless you place it in soil or surround it with the proper nutrients. Quietude and meditation are the same and will not be fruitful unless you provide proper "space" for them to happen. We are growing a smile-garden here! If developing your presence with meditation and prayer is an incidental activity, you will get incidental results. You are worth giving yourself fifteen minutes of uninterrupted space and time—no computer, no email, and the phone is turned off. Many people get stuck by thinking it won't work for them, so they don't even block time in their schedule. Don't let this be you! Make the decision first that you can and will calm yourself and experience quiet time, and then put it on your schedule. If you don't have the time, give yourself five minutes—everyone has at least five uninterrupted minutes!

Quieting your mind right before you sleep is a good way to prepare for a restful night, or first thing in the morning if you have tumultuous dreams—or both! Brief "brain breaks" are powerful during the day as well. Basically, anytime is a good time. Do not worry if you fall asleep during this practice. Just allow the body to take what it needs. If you fall asleep when you meditate or quiet your mind, perhaps you need to invest more in your sleep so that it does not interrupt your practice of turning the brain off. Being chronically sleep-deprived will diminish your ability to be present and will also diminish your smile. We must set aside time to take care of ourselves, replenish, and get enough sleep.

"You should sit in meditation for twenty minutes every day, unless you're too busy. Then you should sit for an hour." — Zen proverb

Can you set aside five to twenty minutes, two to five times per week to pray, be peaceful, and calm your mind? In the afternoon or at the end of the day is a great opportunity because we are usually ready for a break. It is worth repeating, this is no different than exercise. If you never work out, you will not be in shape. If you never take the time to quiet your mind, you will not be calm, relaxed, or even-tempered. Be flexible and persist! This will work for you, don't give up. I promise there is a smile at the end of the tunnel! :)

Physical vs. Emotional Presence: What is Physical Presence?

Alright, you know how to be present, and you may have already set your calendar/reminders/alerts to remind you when to take time to be present. Yet there is another level to explore your presence when the scheduled time to quiet your mind arrives. One of the easiest and most relaxing ways to explore your presence is to just be present with your body and pay attention to your physical senses: sight, sound, touch, smell, and taste. The simplest definition I have found for being present or meditating is "directing your focus towards a specific sensation, feeling, or thought." I like to think of it as a receiving activity or perceiving through the five senses, and not transmitting by talking, thinking, or doing. When you do this correctly, it feels so good that it will bring a smile to your face instantly!

This is your chance to take 100% of the pressure off of yourself. Being present is an opportunity that you can choose to be completely detached in today's "rat race." It's like that feeling of relief when you clock out at the end of the day. Doesn't that make you smile? Honor yourself in the moment by being shiftless and unproductive to a degree that you are amazingly in touch with yourself! Some of you may be saying, "Sounds great, but it isn't so easy for me to turn things off!" I understand, it may take time and practice, but it does work and you will get better the more effort you put into it, especially when you are smiling. Here are the simple ABC's for those beginning with being physically present:

A = **Attention**. Focusing your attention on an object, sensation, chant, sound or your blank-stare smile.

B = **Breathing**. Deep, slow breathing. Feeling each breath is helpful. Sit comfortably, breathe in and out, and count, "1, 2, 3, 4, 5."

C = **Calm**. Lower your heart rate and adrenaline level. Anything that calms you is a step in the right direction.

The ABC's of presence are an act of receiving, just like a radio or satellite TV! Except with being present, you always get all the best channels. :) You are transmitting and not receiving if you are talking or doing or creating new thoughts. When you are receiving, it is almost as if you turn yourself off, and you are just experiencing the world happening to you through your senses. Get a massage, feel your feet as you walk on the ground, taste food you love, listen to sounds that soothe, stop to smell the roses, and gaze at something beautiful. Even if you are chanting (transmitting) when you meditate, you are creating a consistent sound or signal for your ears to hear (receiving). Do you think you can make your body an empty vessel, like a radio receiver with no self, and just experience and receive the world around you? It is a little disorienting to think of no self, though I promise you will come back when the exercise is done. :) When we direct our attention to the five senses (see, hear, touch, taste, and smell), we engage in being physically present. I like to add the sixth sense, the sense of smile. :) You are focusing on your physical body and what you physically feel as opposed to the emotions you are feeling. When we are truly focused on our physical sensations, it feels wonderful and the smile follows naturally.

My brother used to have a fifty-gallon fish tank, and he had the most beautiful fish! It was so tranquil and hypnotic to see them slowly floating and swimming. It was calming to watch the bubbles rise, hear the soft purring of the water filter, and watching the fish food slowly disperse into the water during feeding time. We would turn the lights off in the room and turn the tank light on for the total experience :) It was our fish tank physical meditation! Being present with and watching the fish was so peaceful, we could forget the world around us...and it made us smile. :) What experience makes you smile? Looking at cars, shopping, surrounding yourself with nature? There are so many to choose from!

A fish-tank meditation is an easy place to start finding your smile!

Closing your eyes and slowing your natural breathing can be helpful to deepen your physical presence. But don't fall over or do this when you are driving! When you inhale and exhale slowly, count to five. Focus on the feeling and sound of each breath, and you do your best to not focus on other thoughts. You aren't thinking about bills you have to pay, relationship upsets you may have, or other distractions in your life. You are focused on the sounds, textures, sights, smells, or tastes that you perceive. I feel relaxed just thinking about it...

Meditation and being present usually involve calming or slowing your heart rate and lowering your adrenaline level. Most of the time we are unaware of our heart rate, unless it is beating really fast. If you really want to know how calm you are, you absolutely should measure your heart rate. Hold your fingers on your wrist or place your hand on your chest, and count how many beats you feel in a minute. This practice alone is a great way to calm yourself. Focus on things that make you feel tranquil and at peace. The past is gone forever, and the future only exists in our mind and is not real. All we have is the now, and when we allow ourselves a focused experience without distractions, it can be peaceful and euphoric. Achieving this state of mind is what presence is all about, and it is a brilliant foundation for smiling. :)

Are you using your five senses to find your smile?

Right before you go to bed tonight, think about a time when you were totally focused on one of the senses (physically present) and it felt good, euphoric, or even magical. You can relive the moment right before you drift off into dream land. Can you remember an experience for each of the five senses that allowed you to totally immerse yourself in that sensation? Perhaps a favorite memory from childhood? Or one of your favorite foods or holiday memories? A nice vacation moment? Understanding your body is an enjoyable way to learn and control your smile and facial expressions. Take a few minutes to consider how your physical sensations have created peaceful or special moments involving the senses. Here are a few suggestions below to get you started:

Sight — Look into nature. A tree, a flower, the sky, the rain, or a body of water.

Sound — Listen to your favorite music or to the sounds of nature, focus on what you are listening to and a smile will appear.

Smell — Smell your favorite food, drink, or natural setting and it will often bring back memories that lead to smiling.

Taste — We have thousands of taste buds, find something you can savor and sink your teeth into—especially something that makes you salivate. When you have a great dinner, it makes both you and the chef smile!

Touch — Take a hot bath or shower, focus on the sensation of the water and heat on your skin and body, or give yourself a foot massage. Hugging and physical touch are both very powerful in making us smile. :)

I'm using my sense of taste and my hat to bring out my smile!

Does one of your senses stand out as the strongest? Isn't it powerful to focus on our physical senses? Sometimes we try so hard to block out the distractions from the world around us it can make us numb to the simple pleasures in life. Being present will raise your awareness and sensitivity, which is one of the most direct ways to stimulate your smile When you know how to be present, you can literally take a vacation anytime you want. Nothing is more peaceful and serene than what the present moment has to offer us. It is worth saying again that presence is the greatest present we can ever give or receive.

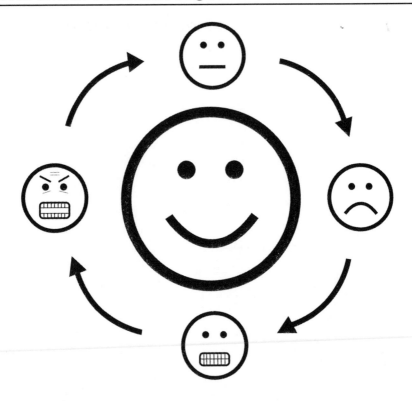

Wouldn't it be GREAT to prevent the negative distractions in life from disrupting your 'presence' and stealing your smile? Well now you can when you practice Emotional Presence!

Emotional Presence

In my humble opinion, this is what I believe and find to be true in my practice and in my life: physical presence is powerful, but what has more impact is emotional presence. When I started being more emotionally present, I started to understand what really makes me tick. Emotional presence is about our feelings. When we feel tense or stressed, many times we can be unaware of this tension. Some people will totally deny what they are feeling. Am I getting too touchy-feely here? Alright, I will break down emotional presence into two physical ingredients: your smile and your heart rate. Check out my fancy diagram that explains our emotional presence.

Emotional IQ & Emotional Presence: The Four Quadrants

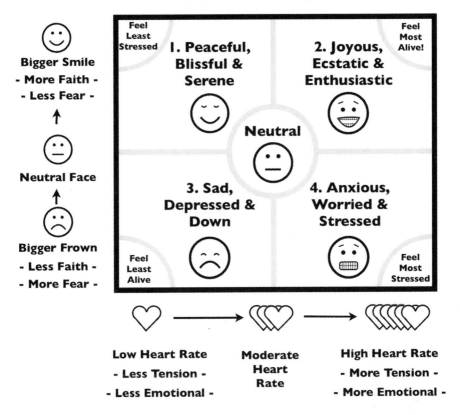

This is just a simple diagram to get you thinking about how your body responds when you have different emotions. Please don't get too specific on details right now, this is a generalization to activate awareness about your emotions. So what does all of this mean?

Quadrant 1 happens when we feel peaceful, serene, and blissful, where we are smiling and our heart rate is low (feel least stressed).

Quadrant 2 is someone who is joyful, ecstatic, and enthusiastic, and they are smiling with a high heart rate (feel most alive).

Quadrant 3 reveals that when we are sad, depressed, and down, we display a frown and have a low heart rate (feel most depressed).

Quadrant 4 happens when we are anxious, worried, or stressed, and our frown is accompanied by a high heart rate (feel most stressed).

Now, why are these four quadrants important? Because they show some consistent patterns that practically all human beings demonstrate. And, it is very difficult to express an emotion when your body is in an opposite quadrant. For example, you can't be peaceful and serene (Quadrant 1) when you are frowning and your heart is racing (Quadrant 4), just as it is hard be worried (Quadrant 4) when you show a genuine smile and your heart rate is low (Quadrant 1). And, when we are smiling and our heart is beating fast (Quadrant 2), it is difficult to be depressed (Quadrant 3), just as it is difficult to be joyful and ecstatic (Quadrant 2) when we are frowning and have a low heart rate (Quadrant 3). So Quadrants 1 and 4 are opposites, just as Quadrants 2 and 3 are opposite as well. Of course, there are exceptions to every rule, though these generalizations hold true most of the time. High and low heart rate are relative, with the normal range being from 60-90 beats per minute. Just place your hand on your heart to feel your resting heart rate. This way you can tell when your heart is beating fast or slow. And we certainly know when our heart is racing, right? If someone cuts us off while driving on the highway, or the bad guy jumps out of the shadows in a horror film, we can relate to what it feels like when our heart is beating fast.

I love this diagram because I have found many lessons directly applicable for myself and those I care most about. The more I consider the four quadrants, it seems that our body responds predictably and clearly when we display different emotions. The next time you are in a stressful situation, ask yourself what quadrant you are in. I do this all the time, especially when I feel frustrated at the office or at home. When I realize I am in Quadrant 4, I take a deep breath and try to lower my heart rate and find something to smile about. If we want to change how we feel, we have to change our behavior and our meanings, and our emotions will follow. For example, if I am feeling down, I move my body as much as I can. Raising my arms up above my head (raise your hands up in the air!) and exerting myself will raise my heart rate and move me from Quadrants 1 or 3 to Quadrants 2 or 4. Try it for yourself and see how powerful this can be. It is easy to see that we feel most alive when are in Quadrant 2 (joyous, ecstatic, and enthusiastic), and least alive when we are in Quadrant 3 (sad, depressed, and down). Our behaviors tend to be a comfortable pattern we follow, acting out our feelings from the quadrant we are in. If we want to change our behavior and change quadrants, we simply redirect what we are focusing on to determine what quadrant our emotions go to next. What is really fun is knowing that the higher my heart rate goes, the more emotional I will feel, just as lowering my heart rate will lessen my emotional intensity.

I'm smiling and calming myself down so I can be in Quadrant 1.

I'm smiling and I'm really excited - it feels GREAT to be in Quadrant 2

My heart rate and smile are low and I'm in Quadrant 3.

Quadrant 4, my heart rate is HIGH and my smile is LOW!

Can you see how these quadrants fit into your life and daily routine? Have you ever finished your day of work, school, or taking care of the family, and felt tense, tired, or both? Did this ever result in you snapping at someone you care about? Maybe you are close to Quadrant 4, and don't realize it. This happened to me all the time when I did not acknowledge and tend to my emotions. It is so easy to be emotionally absent, which is the opposite of being emotionally present. It was ruining my life and almost destroyed my marriage. I finally realized how to be present with myself and my emotions. Emotional presence and smiling have made all the difference in my life, and I know it will make a difference for you too!

When I was in Quadrant 4 in the past, all I knew was that I didn't like how I felt, and I would try to escape this feeling or quadrant with any activity I could find nearby. It was easy to go to the Internet or TV, hoping it would make me smile, or help me to lower my heart rate. This strategy of avoiding my emotions worked in the short term, just as it usually failed in the long run, because escaping is only treating the symptoms of how I felt and not the root cause. The problem with these diversions is that they stopped me from listening to my body and my emotions. My emotions may have been saying, "I'm tired, weary, fearful, stressed out, and I need comforting." But I didn't realize what I was feeling and what I really needed both physically and emotionally. Now, when I recognize what quadrant I am in, I can proactively change how I feel rather than just reacting to what I am feeling in the moment.

If you are going to use and apply this in your life, you must be a great listener to what your body is saying. When your body tells you something, you should listen to it! Be aware of what quadrant you are in (or near), and if you need to disengage from what you are doing to be more aware with your body, change your heart rate, or change your smile. Meditate, take a nap, take a walk, rest your eyes, and get in touch with your emotional presence. It is too easy of a distraction to surf the net, check e-mail, text, browse Facebook, or do all of these things at the same time! The Internet is no substitute for real live relationships! Do not fall into the social media trap when you are overtired! Brainless browsing can leave you more tense afterward because it is not relaxing, and actually steals your time and brings your smile down! Being present with YouTube videos is not a great strategy for saving your relationships!

So when you explore your emotional presence, think about whether your heart rate is high or low, and whether or not you are smiling or frowning. Does this put you in the quadrant you thought you were in or want to be in? Are you spending time with the people and things that matter most to you? And when you do spend that time, are you getting excited and sharing your smile towards the things that are most important? Sometimes we show up in a quadrant that is not congruent with what we want, and when that happens, we have to start working on changing our smile and our heart rate! Emotional presence helps us to be in charge of how and when we smile. :-)

Do you see how your emotions can fit into these categories? In our world, many people are oblivious to their emotions. Take the time to be emotionally present with yourself to see and feel who you are and where you are with your smile and your heart rate. Physical and emotional presence is the solution for anyone who wants to enhance their smile. When you quiet your mind on a regular basis, you will see your challenges gradually lose their power over you. So let's get started being present! I'm so excited about this I am literally freaking out (Quadrant 2)! Okay, while I am breathing deeply and getting a hold of myself in an attempt to lower my heart rate, here is a story I like to tell of a patient of mine that was in great need of practicing her emotional presence.

Samantha the Stylist: The story of a self-conscious smile (Quadrant 4)

Samantha is a hairdresser and a makeup artist in her mid-forties who helps people look and feel good about themselves! When I met her for the first time, she did not smile very easily and was nervous. You can not help but notice how she is very attentive to detail when it comes to her personal appearance. She keeps herself in good athletic shape, and keeps her curly brown hair with highlights tied back with a stylish hair-band. I was trying to guess what she could possibly want from me, she didn't seem to need much of anything! But, I asked her what I ask all of my patients, "How can I help you? To me, you look terrific! What specifically are you looking to achieve?"

She reluctantly looked in the mirror, "Ugghh! I HATE how I look, I need a facelift!" She went on to point out numerous specific and different areas and flaws she wanted to address as her face was inches away from her reflection. By most people's standards, she was an attractive woman, though she certainly didn't feel that way about herself. The areas she pointed out were visible and noticeable only when you were right up close to her face. Many of her concerns could be considered invisible in social situations, and they did not dominate her facial appearance. She was right in the middle of Quadrant 4 (high heart rate, low smile = STRESS), and her extreme attention to detail made her irritable about her appearance! She was being too hard on herself, and she snapped at me "Oh, my face...it looks like a dog's rear-end!"

I reacted, "Samantha! Now be nice..."

She continued, "No, really, I do look terrible! Don't just tell me what you tell everyone!" Samantha became emotional and went on to say, "I never really feel pretty, and I'm not happy. In fact, I never let anyone take pictures of me because I don't like how I look when I smile!" She started to cry, and I handed her a box of tissues. Her comments and constant criticisms of her appearance were clear evidence that she had a low self-image. She really wanted to feel prettier, but did not know how. She did not know that our sense of self-worth and self-love are something we create inside of us, regardless of our actual appearance. My compliment confused her, and she did not see her beauty.

I see this all too often in my office. People will say the most awful things about themselves. We tell ourselves things we would never say to another person, and we rationalize that it is okay to disrespect ourselves because these words come from us. Well, they don't come from us, they come from words someone else said to us many years ago, and I call this voice our "inner bully."

I started working to expand her perspective, make her smile, and move her into Quadrant 1 or 2. "Okay, Samantha, why don't you show me your smile!" She made a half-effort at a smile and I coached her, "Thank you, that is one-half of a smile, keep it coming, keep it coming, *you are getting closer*...there it is!!!" She flashed a real smile (Quadrant 2) for just a fraction of a second, before she slipped back into her blank, almost frowning face of Quadrant 4.

We talked about how we never see ourselves the way others see us. We look at the mirror and judge ourselves when we wear a flat expression, yet we are never expressionless when we talk to others. We look waaaaaaayyyy better when we are animated with facial expressions. If we want to see ourselves the way that others see us, we need to watch a video of ourselves, or make facial expressions while we are looking at ourselves in the mirror. When our face is in motion, the imperfections melt away and are invisible. I gave her this explanation, but these words didn't really do much to make her feel better about herself.

> *"Oh would some power the gift to give us to see ourselves as others see us." — Robert Burns*

I knew I had to be very careful about what I said next. I paused and took the time to be fully present with her. I said to her, with as much caring and compassion as I could, "Samantha, you are a beautiful woman, and many of our patients would love to trade places with you." Even though every word is true, she gives me a look of disbelief. "And you are hard on yourself. So many people say mean things to themselves, things that they would never say to other people, yet often feel it is okay because it came from their own head. I call this our inner bully."

She responded, "I can't help it, I am around other make-up artists, and we are always picking out people's flaws, including our own!!! I may say harsh things about my face, but they are all true!"

"Okay, I hear you. So let me ask you a question. With or without flaws, do you know the most attractive thing we do to our face?" I ask her.

"What?" as she waits for this facial miracle.

I demonstrated on my face and point to my cheeks. "A smile! We look most attractive when we smile. We literally attract people to us when we smile." I asked her to look into the mirror and smile. She put on a self-conscious smile, and I rolled my sleeves up and looked in the mirror with her as I flash a big smile right at her. This put her over the top, and we shared a smile together. *Finally!!* "See, doesn't that look good? We get compliments on our smile, and our smile makes us feel good about ourselves. Nothing I can do will make you look as attractive as your smile does. I am happy to help you with some of these areas of facial aging, though we must keep a healthy perspective on what is realistic and what will look natural."

We talked for a while, and Samantha told me, "It makes me feel better to hear you say that, and I do appreciate how you care for your patients. Though, I'm still have trouble feeling that way on my own."

I told her, "That is completely normal. The voices in your head have been pointing out imperfections for a long time now, they don't just turn off overnight." I gave her some smiling homework to practice in the mirror, and I told her she needed to have faith in the process and in my professional advice. For someone who didn't like their smile, you could see she was already smiling more warmly and genuinely (Quadrant 1 and 2). It was touching to see someone looking in the mirror at themselves and seeing their own true beauty, and she didn't need any treatments to make that happen!

Samantha left our consultation and gave me a big hug and a big smile. I said, "You don't need a facelift, we can do some facial fillers after we work on your smile. I am going to be checking up on you, and the next time you come in, don't tell me the dog ate your smile homework." I also cautioned her, "Please make sure that you don't smile *too* much. I cannot be held responsible for any happiness you experience above and beyond what you are used to!" This made her smile even more. She was going for extra-credit on her smile homework!

What does the bully in your head say to you? Do you ever say things to yourself that you would NEVER say to someone else? You must be present with yourself to hear how the inner bully can say things that steal our smile.

Everyone Hates Bullies, Yet Most Play One in Their Mind

Samantha's inner bully may have been getting the best of her, but her smile helped her to stand up to the bully and declare her self-worth. Do you know of anyone that is hard on themselves, or perhaps says mean things to themselves? I know I am guilty of this. Emotional presence will help us to see and feel where we are bullied in life. Often we subconsciously nitpick ourselves. Many people I know have an inner voice that nags and bullies them. "You're too late. You're too fat. You don't look good enough. You sound stupid. You are clumsy. You are doing this wrong. You aren't going to make it. You are too slow..." and so on. I was speaking with a friend recently, and he told me, "If someone treated me the same way the voice in my head treats me, I'd kill him." One day

108

I caught my inner bully red-handed. I was walking from my car to my house, carrying way too much stuff in both of my arms. I got halfway to the house, and I dropped my water bottle. No big deal, right? Wrong. My inner voice pounced on me in a split second. "You STUPID IDIOT!" rang out in my head. I have quietly berated myself for minor clumsiness as long as I can remember. The first time I was emotionally present and actually realized I was saying this, I paused and laughed. I thought to myself, "Come on! It's just a water bottle, get over it, make one more trip, what is the big deal, don't beat yourself up so much!" We often do not realize the frequency and intensity of the negative things we may say inside our head. Our inner bully can keep us afraid of being judged by the outside world, imprisoning us in the stress of Quadrant 4. Allowing our inner bully to run free will absolutely take away from our inner smile and prevent us from smiling and existing in Quadrants 1 or 2.

In my office, if a patient is disrespectful to themselves or allows their inner bully to run free, I take the time to interject and set some ground rules. "I hear what you are saying, though we have a rule here that you have to be nice to yourself. You would never say those words to another person, right?"

"No I wouldn't," they say.

"Okay, let's be nice to you. No one deserves to be spoken to that way, even if it is yourself. Agreed?"

Most people agree with me, because no one likes a bully. Yet so many people bully themselves. Why do we beat ourselves up this way?

We hear these thoughts and think it is acceptable because they come from our own head. Yet we would never let someone else say those same words to us. This is bullying, plain and simple. What gives? We shouldn't stand for that. Why do we think it is okay when negativity comes from our own head? I was completely unaware I made these bullying comments to myself, and I was constantly allowing myself to feel bad over these little bombs of nitpicking negativity. The inner voice incessantly whispered these guilt-trips that kept adding up until I felt frustrated, upset, or physically ill.

What is more, these negative thoughts don't initially come from us. They often come from times we were hurt in the past. It could be anything really. Something someone said about our physical appearance or intelligence. Perhaps a time when we were clumsy in a crowded room. Sometimes it is completely made up and fabricated, but we can still be convinced it is true. When I was a kid walking around on crutches, I was called, "cripple" and "lame" and I got into fights defending my self-confidence from bullies. Now, that memory has the power to act like an inner bully. It may never go away if I secretly agree with it and feed it. Yes, we may be a little clumsy, or we may be a little overweight, or we may be embarrassed if we don't know something. But much of the time these tiny inner-complaints are BALONEY! Even if the statements aren't true, if we agree with them on a subconscious level, the inner bullying will continue.

We must stand up, recognize, and confront these bully-memories, but not as a bully ourselves. We should befriend our inner bully. Once we bring our inner bully out into the light, then you can see how to work with the bully and show them that we won't stand down. If our inner bully tells us that we are ugly, we must stand the bully down and declare that we are beautiful. What if the bully says something accurate, like we are out of shape? We must proclaim to the bully that we have great strength inside, and we can and will overcome this. You can not allow the bully to tell you who you are and what you can or cannot do, and more importantly, we cannot allow the bully to tell us how to feel. We must guard our emotions like a vulnerable child that needs to be protected from those that wish to do us harm and take advantage of us. Stop allowing the inner bully to feed our mind negative garbage. If you have a thought that is negative garbage, throw it out just like any other garbage.

Are you willing to stand up to your inner bully? And who is that bully? It is usually someone nameless and of no consequence, yet they are very real in our subconscious. Often they are no longer in our lives. Most of the time they were a passing relationship, or a friend or family member that got a good insult in on us. These negative memories will never go away until we replace them with a more empowering meaning.

I have met a few people that have honestly told me they do not talk to themselves using harsh or mean words. This is very uncommon. Be honest with yourself and listen to what your inner bully says to you that demeans you or makes you feel bad about yourself. When you know how to listen and not take it personally, it is actually much more fun to befriend our inner bully and not live in fear of the constant criticism. If you give yourself a harsh inner comment that does not make you happy with your appearance, you can come back and say, "I may not be perfect, but I still look great." Or if your inner voice complains that you are not in shape or living a healthy lifestyle, reply with, "I may not be in the best shape now, but I am going to take care of myself and restore my health and fitness!" We should be prepared and practiced for what we can say to overcome negative self-talk, and then we must follow through on those actions.

Now let's show that bully who is boss. It is your head after all, isn't it? The next time they show up and whisper negativity in your ear, you will be ready! You will knock them for a loop and they will lose power over you when you are prepared and you defend your self-worth. But you must first take the time to be emotionally present and listen carefully to your inner dialogue. Ultimately, we create the inner voices in our head by who we listen to, and what we feel is important. Our thoughts and emotions are just like little kids. They absorb everything from external influences. Just like children, you must spend time and be present with your thoughts and emotions if you want them to be healthy, well cared for and productive. If our thoughts and emotions cross the line and become too negative, we have to lovingly steer them back to where they need to be!

Standing up to your inner bully is not hard to do once you shine a light on it when you are emotionally present. When you are aware, you can redefine what your inner bully is saying. With emotional presence, befriending and taming your inner bully is easy. When you see that you have nothing to fear, and when your bully realizes you will not give in, this realization will make you stronger. There is often a grain of truth in what your inner bully may say, but that does not mean it has to be negative. Your internal dialogue can be used to your advantage as long as you keep your focus on the positive and you do not allow it to bring you down. Letting your inner bully run free will definitely dampen your ability to smile. Emotional presence allows us to be aware of and befriend our inner bully. Lack of emotional presence and an overbearing inner bully are some of the top reasons people do not give themselves permission to enjoy life and smile more freely.

Which voices do you hear in your head the positive or the negative?

**Are you showing the negative voices who is boss?
When you are emotionally present and aware of your
inner bullies, they can become your friends
and advisors.**

So, when you took the time to be present with your emotions, did you find anything hiding inside of you? Did your emotional presence make you feel calm (Q1), anxious and tense (Q4), depressed (Q3), excited (Q2), or happy (Q 1 & 2)? If you feel nothing at all, that is okay. Be patient and keep listening and feeling, it will come to you. When you are open, you will find it. If you are like me, you find that there are a lot of things that upset you when you stop smiling for too long! I will start to fuss about silly things: "This is too hot, or too cold! Someone said something I don't like! Things didn't turn out the way I had planned!" When we are overtired or pushed to our limit, we can sometimes act like a toddler melting down. Trust me when I say that putting a smile on our face makes it harder for the "inner toddler" to melt-down.

Take the Time to Be Emotionally Present

I like to think about emotions like they are family. We should welcome them, whether they are positive or negative :) Give them the respect they deserve, and greet them as if you are greeting someone very special. These emotions came from you and are just like your family because they are a part of you. But do not try to act on your emotions just yet. Be present with them. With time, the correct action for you to take will become obvious, and usually there is no hurry to address what is stirring our emotions. After all, we have let our emotions wait this long, haven't we?

Now that you have mastered physical and emotional presence, give yourself a pat on the back! It feels good to know ourselves better, don't you agree? Before we go to the next chapter, let me ask you a question: Have you ever wanted to read someone's thoughts or know what they are thinking? Chapter 4 will assist you knowing and understanding your environment and surroundings so well, you will actually be able to predict the preferences of others and anticipate their needs before they say one word. And when you know what people want, you have great power in making them SMILE!

As a kid, emotional presence meant crying when upset, lashing out when I was angry, and smiling only when I felt happy. With *The Smile Prescription*, I still have feelings, but now I am in control :)

DOCTOR'S ORDERS:

1. Embrace meditation, quietude, and being present to improve your health and your smile.

2. Changing your thoughts leads to a change your behaviors, which will change your brain.

3. Focus on your senses to achieve physical presence.

4. Focus on your feelings, heart rate, and smile to achieve emotional presence.

5. Make friends with your inner bully, and don't be afraid to learn from the negative voices.

6. Be aware if your self-talk is positive or negative.

SMILE REFLECTIONS:

- How does it feel to focus on the simple things in life?

- What most impacts you when you are present and/or meditating?

- Do you know of anyone that could benefit from meditation or being more present?

- The best way to help others be more present is to be more present yourself.

chapter four

READING FACES TELLS YOU EVERYTHING

"Happiness, trust, friendship, love... You can tell all of these things and so much more about a person from their smile." — Dr. Rich

"A smile cures the wounding of a frown." — William Shakespeare

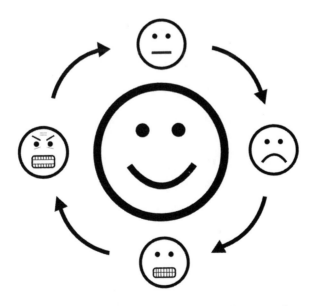

Who or what is in your smile environment? We tend to make the same faces as those we spend the most time with.

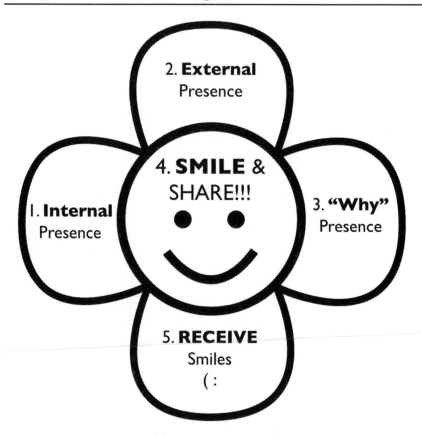

The Smile Blossom: Five Easy Steps to Making Anyone's Smile Bloom

Step 1: Be present internally. Develop the presence of your "Smile Bud." Listen to and focus on understanding your body and yourself.

Step 2: Be present externally. Unfold your petals, expand your presence and focus, and be open to your environment and those people around you.

Step 3: Be present with your "Why." Pollinate your world with empowering meaning.

Step 4: SMILE and have fun with it! Enjoy your flowering beauty and create a bouquet of smiles by helping friends and family to smile with you.

Step 5: Receive and complete the cycle of happiness with a "Thank You." Validate and encourage others to grow their smile blossoms, smile bouquets, and happiness.

Are you ready for the travel experience of a lifetime? We are going to revisit your external world: the environment and faces that you choose for your work and home life. You will see your surroundings as you have never seen them before! This next chapter is wonderful for building teamwork and anticipating the needs of your family, friends, and coworkers. Now that you are able to tune into your physical body and your emotions, it is much easier to learn and understand those around you. If you know what you are looking for, you can read people like a book. :) It is definitely worthwhile to reread portions of chapter three to let those lessons sink in, as they will certainly help you build your smile foundation. Being present and giving yourself quiet time are lifelong habits that will continue to grow with you and bring great peace and meaning to your life and to your smile.

Once we know the benefits of smiling and being present, what are the best ways to engage these life-altering practices with the world around us? You must choose your environment and the people you surround yourself with very carefully. We tend to make the same faces as those we spend the most time with. How do you know if you are putting yourself in the right environment and the right peer group to bring out your smile? We think about peer pressure as a grade school phenomenon, but it never really goes away. One day when my daughter got home from school, I asked her how she dealt with the peer pressure that day.

"What are you talking about?" she said.

"Well, you know, with peer pressure, you are either doing the influencing, or you are being influenced. So which did you do today?"

She rolled her eyes and said, "Daaaadddd…"

I figure that it will sink in over time.

I love the old saying, "Look around the poker table; if you can't see the sucker, you're it!" So, are you the one influencing your peers' smile, or are they influencing your smile? Be honest with yourself. If you don't know who is doing the influencing, then you are the one being influenced (the sucker)! This chapter will focus on how to be present with and assess your environment, and how to be present on a deeper level with the people that you choose to make important in your life. This will allow you to be more purposeful about how you use your influence and how you allow yourself to be influenced. When we are in greater control of what influences us, we are in greater control of our smile and our happiness.

"SORRY, SMILE'S OFF..."

**Everywhere we go, influence is happening.
We are either influencing, being influenced, or both!**

Is Your Environment Stealing Your Smile?

One of my favorite things in life is being a parent. :-) When raising children, you learn that a chaotic environment will set them up for failure. Order and structure promote growth while chaos and lack of boundaries are counterproductive. You can't play tennis, basketball, football, volleyball, or soccer if there is stuff strewn all over the playing field or court. You can't cook a great meal when the kitchen is a mess. And the same is with the game of life. It is much harder to smile and be present when you are surrounded with mess and chaos. Even if your baseline environment is not organized or clean, at least recognize that it isn't, and prioritize that you either need to fix it or get a new environment to work or play in.

I love my parents, but both of them had a tendency to hoard. When I was growing up, we went through phases of cleanliness, though we always had rooms

118

or closets that were full to the brim of stuff that sat there. We would excavate our junk and, like archeologists, marvel at the things from our past. Of course, when we wanted to find things, we absolutely could not because it was trapped in the clutter. Clutter = Stress = No Smile.

My kids can be untidy, and usually once per day I am searching the entire house for lost clothes, toys, books, or other items of importance. I like being the hero and saving the day for my kids, but it would be a lot less stressful and save time for everyone if we were all a bit more organized with our space and our things. For life and relationships to grow, we need a clean and organized play space and workspace. It is not surprising that the industry of space-planners and organizers has grown large in our modern society. Everyone needs help in keeping clean, organized, and unfettered as we take on our daily challenges. Make being tidy a priority, and it will support the smiling and happiness of you and those around you.

What Are the Ingredients That Make Up Your Environment?

As soon as you enter a room or space, your subconscious mind immediately picks up what is present in that space. Take a moment to feel the energy of the space you are in. Noisy or quiet? Chaotic or ordered? Comfortable or uncomfortable? Smelly or Clean? From the sense of taste, you can ask if the food in this environment tastes good, bad, or is healthy or unhealthy. These simple guidelines tell you if the space you are in is favorable for smiling and engaging with others. Too much clutter can distract our presence. Just think about how people respond when they walk into a room and see a big mess. Usually they are uncomfortable, and it actually wipes the smile off their face.

It is worth repeating, are the unhappy faces in your environment stealing your smile?

Virtual Mind-Reading in Your Environment

Being present in your environment with others will reveal who or what is helping or hurting your smile. If you spend enough time with someone, you will learn there is no hiding who you really are. We may fool ourselves in the short term, but over time you will easily see who makes you happy and who doesn't.

"Who you are speaks so loudly I can't hear what you're saying." — Ralph Waldo Emerson

When I meet people I can immediately tell who the smilers and the non-smilers are. In just a few seconds, all you have to do is shine your smile on someone to see how they respond. They will either match, exceed, or not return your energy. With few exceptions, this is an accurate indicator of how readily someone smiles.

You can easily tell who the frequent smilers are in the same manner you learn how good someone is at throwing a frisbee. If you want to know how good someone is at playing frisbee, just throw a frisbee at them! If they catch it and throw it right back to you, they are usually pretty good. If they hesitate a little, perhaps fumble a

Is your environment lifting you up?!?

bit or drop it, and then throw it back to you, they are probably an average frisbee thrower. If they let it drop at their feet and ignore it or leave it there, chances are they don't throw frisbee that much. It is very similar with people when you throw your smile at them.

For example, I like to throw a "smile frisbee" and make an uplifting comment. "Great to see you!" or "So glad you're here!" If I get a smile back quickly, it's a good indication that they are a frequent smiler. As the conversation continues, positive people will perk up and return a positive facial expression or comment. "Yes, we had a great time this weekend," or "So good to see you as well!" If you receive a weak response, or no response at all, then this person is less likely to be a frequent smiler. There is usually some source of pain that prevents someone from smiling frequently. Now, people smile for all kinds of reasons. Not always for the happy ones. Sometimes you can get someone to smile by joining them in a mini pity-party. For example, if you start complaining, there are some people that will enjoy complaining with you, and it will make them smile. Have you ever heard the saying, "Misery loves company"? Everyone has negativity in their life somewhere, and it is okay to be there and be genuine and real with what bothers you. Just don't get stuck there for too long :)

One day I was performing a treatment for a gentleman, and I told him, "Everything is going fine!" He snapped at me, "You tell that to everyone, just tell me what you are doing and save me the baloney!" Whoa, how did he get so bent out of shape? I didn't want this to be a bad experience for him, and I love to keep people comfortable by having them smile. So I went into my "misery loves company" mode and started complaining about how my kids ruin everything we have in our house. In milliseconds, he resonated with this negativity as he flashed a smile and started sharing, "Oh yeah, wait until they start driving your cars! My kids all crashed their cars the first year they were driving, you just wait until your insurance rates go crazy!" Even though we were complaining, the conversation made us smile!

Being present with others is like being present with yourself. You must only shift your focus and decide that this is a person that you want to know well. Are you interested in this person? Why is it important that you know this person or these people well? What is your favorite thing that you absolutely love about this special human being? After all, they are someone's son or daughter or family member. What is a genuine compliment you can give about something special you see in them? Can you find something to be their number one fan about? Questions will help you feel curious and learn more about anyone you connect with. The more you get to know someone the easier it is to smile with them!

Everyone you meet is someone's baby or loved one! There is always a good reason to be present with or get to know some one better (:

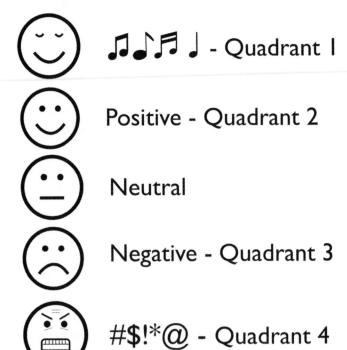

♫♪♬ ♩ - Quadrant 1

Positive - Quadrant 2

Neutral

Negative - Quadrant 3

#$!*@ - Quadrant 4

You can read how positive or negative someone's thoughts are by their facial expression. It is very difficult to keep positive or negative thinking or feelings from showing on our face (: Refer to chapter three's Emotional Intelligence Chart.

Quadrant 1 happens when we feel peaceful, serene, and blissful, where we are smiling and our heart rate is low (feel least stressed).

Quadrant 2 is someone who is joyful, ecstatic, and enthusiastic, and they are smiling with a high heart rate (feel most alive).

Quadrant 3 reveals that when we are sad, depressed, and down, we display a frown and have a low heart rate (feel most depressed).

Quadrant 4 happens when we are anxious, worried, or stressed, and our frown is accompanied by a high heart rate (feel most stressed).

Choosing an environment with a merry-go-round usually makes us smile (:

Why Do We Choose Our Environment and Our Peers?

Wherever you choose to be, make sure you know why you are there. When it comes to where you live, work, or play, sometimes we end up in places that do not serve us. I like to ask questions about my environment. For example, do I feel good energy when I enter the room? Why or why not? What is special about this place, and who are the special people here? If you were complimenting this place or the people here, what would you say to them? What do you want to learn more about from these people or this environment? Based on how you respond to these questions, it will be clear if an environment or peer group will support you or bring you down. Where are the places and who are the people that help you to smile the most?

Deep-Dive: Going Beyond the Surface with Your Presence

When we are being present with someone, we observe them. We listen to everything they say. So how do we take being present to a deeper level yet, without someone feeling like we are staring at them or treating them like an object? The secret is to create trust and maintain rapport! This will allow them to open up and express themselves more. And the best way to create trust and build rapport is through smiling. This will deepen what we share and enhance our ability to listen and understand. When you have trust and rapport with someone, you hold the power to make them smile.

When you truly know what someone wants, you hold the power to make them smile. Just as when you know what makes someone smile, you know what they truly want. Conversely, if you don't know what someone wants, it is much harder to make them smile.

Ask a kid if they want candy and see if it makes them smile. If you want them to smile even bigger, ask them if they really, really want the candy, and then ask how will they feel if they eat the candy. Sooner or later, a smile will pop up, and that means you know they want that candy! And giving them that candy starts to build your trust in the relationship.

Playing "copy-cat" with kids will definitely bring out your smile!

I like to play "copy-cat" with my kids, nephews, and nieces. Whatever position they are holding their body in, I do the same and see if I can get them to notice. I stand the way they stand, and walk the exact way they walk, in step with them if possible. I say what they say, in the same high pitched voice (maybe a bit exaggerated for effect), just so I can have fun with them and get them to smile. I just love poking fun at my kids and family! When I get home at the end of the day, if my kids are playing on the floor, I get down and play with them. If they are running around the house, I chase them and they chase me. If you approach any child and start copying and mirroring their behaviors and movements in a playful way (with a smile on your face), that alone will usually make them smile. If they are playing with cars and making "VROOM VROOM" noises, you do the same. If they are pouring tea for their stuffed animals, get on your knees and be the waiter. But can you really do this for adults? The answer is yes. But we have to be more subtle to make it work. For example, if they are standing, stand the way they do and hold yourself in a similar manner. When someone talks quietly, you do the same. This is also known as "mirroring" someone, because you are acting like their reflection in the mirror. If they are speaking loudly and in an animated fashion, follow suit and it will bring you closer to them. Eat what they are eating, drink what they are drinking, and do what they are doing, and that will create rapport with your body language. :)

The establishing of trust and rapport is an important part of *The Smile Prescription*. So what is "trust and rapport with body language?" Who do we trust? We trust people who are like ourselves, from the first moment we come in contact with another person we are making conscious and unconscious discriminations that determine whether they are like us or not. So lead with your best smile. Rapport is an automatic agreement built from anything you share in common with someone. When it comes to rapport with body language, that means sharing in common the posture, mannerisms, energy, and facial expressions of whomever you are communicating with. If I am around kids, it is easy to build rapport with them by just acting, talking, singing, and moving my body the way they do. Some feel self-conscious that building rapport with body language is obvious and will be seen as fake or insincere. Most people are totally unaware of when you are mirroring them, and even if they are aware, if you are sincerely interested in learning about them or helping them, they often appreciate you even more. Practice makes perfect! Try the "mirroring game" with the next person you are talking with. You will be amazed how they don't realize what you are doing. After a few moments, you will start to recognize how you understand their mood better when you share their energy level and how they move their body. It is fun creating this foundation for smiling!

Conversational Rapport Builds Smiles

Rapport is built conversationally as well, and it is any connection or thing you share in common with someone else. Rapport is the glue of any good relationship. One of the best definitions of conversational rapport is getting someone else to say, "Me too!" If you can elicit or give a genuine "Me Too!" response to any circumstance or situation, you are building rapport. "You love golf? Me Too!" or, "I love eating at that restaurant too!" :) or, "You bought that shirt online? I have ordered from the same place!" I know, I know, if you are just saying "Me Too!" all the time, people get the picture that you are not being sincere. However, when you authentically find things you share in common with someone else, you will start to form a bond that is undeniable, and, it will make you both smile. :) Another form of conversational rapport building is getting someone to say "Yes!" When you can get someone to say "Yes" to what you are saying or doing, that shows that you share something in common. Even a "No" can build rapport if it is something you are both saying "No" to. "Oh yeah, I *hate* eating that kind of food too, I will never go to that restaurant!" If two people say "No" to the same thing, they have rapport. Rapport can be created in any situation, activity, or experience, even if it is in your past or in your future. Here are just a few categories you can build rapport with:

1. Body Language

2. Energy/Adrenaline/Heart Rate

3. Vocabulary

4. Food and Drink

5. Activities/Culture/Age

6. Religion/Politics

7. Technology

8. Fashion

9. Hygiene

10. Music/Dance

When you build effective rapport, people remember you. They will remember the feeling that they like you and they will have a reason to talk to you again. Let's go through these common areas of rapport to be clear about how this is a very important tool of communication.

Body Language - When you build rapport, your words are always *less important* than how you are present with your body. Make sure you use good body language to make a person feel listened to and understood. Body language also reflects energy levels. Are they sitting or standing at attention? Are they slouching or do they have good posture? Interested or disinterested? Powerful or weak? This is the easiest way to start building rapport, even though some may feel self-conscious about observing the body posture and habits of a person they are in a conversation with. It takes less than a second to observe someone's body language, and you can naturally mirror them to make sure you are sharing as much in common as possible. At first, you may think it is too noticeable when you copy someone's physical posture or behaviors. The truth is that people don't really pay that much attention to us on a conscious level, so you are safe when you use the mirroring technique!

Siblings building rapport on the sofa.

Energy/Adrenaline - to match someone's adrenaline level, you must realize if they are excited and what they are excited about. How do they hold their body, what are they paying attention to, and where is their focus? Make sure you are focusing on the same thing together with the same intensity.

Vocabulary - Make it a point to use the same keywords with whomever you are building rapport with. If they are interested in a particular name, or animal, or business, then repeat that word. Resist the temptation to rephrase what someone says in words that are very different if you can illustrate your point using the words they use. When you talk like a child to a college professor, or talk like a professor to a group of kids, you are likely to break rapport using very unfamiliar language.

Activities/Culture/Age - Sharing the same hobbies, cultural background, or even growing up around the same time can bring a lot of rapport to the relationship. Having a friend or family member that shares a similar interest, heritage, or generation can help you build rapport in a conversation.

Religion/Politics - This is a touchy subject, yet if you share something in common here it can be a very powerful way to get close to one another. Tread lightly, and don't be judgmental. Look for things you enjoy and can celebrate about one another.

Technology - Do you have the same smartphone or computer as the person you are talking to? Do you use the same applications or software? Are one of you totally computer literate while the other is computer illiterate? Do you see the similarities in how you use technology?

Fashion - Do you dress the same? High-fashion or no-fashion? Warm or cool? Leisure wear or professional? Details matter… Or, if the details don't matter to either one of you then you will build rapport in this category. :)

Hygiene - Someone who is a clean freak may not get along well with someone who doesn't brush their teeth or wash their hands frequently, and vice versa.

Music/Dance - Music can bring people together, and it can drive some people away. It is okay to have different music tastes. If you do, can you find something you like about another person's music taste even if you don't enjoy the same music?

Food and Drink - Vegetarians share rapport in their eating habits, as do those who enjoy eating at a steakhouse. Find out why people have their food preferences if you want to build rapport and get to know them better.

If you are a donkey, you share in rapport with other donkeys!

Strengthening Rapport with Compliments

Once you start building rapport, you can strengthen this bond by celebrating someone's special traits or qualities. If you can pay a genuine compliment to someone about something you share in common, you will considerably elevate your status in their eyes. Of course, compliments must be real and truthful. Never lie to make a compliment. Even if you do connect with someone through a lie, it is temporary and detrimental as true feelings always come out sooner or later. Try on a few of these compliments:

- I really love the energy you have for _____. Where do you get your inspiration for that?

- Nice hair/outfit! My friend/wife/sister has the same style as you. You would get along great with one another. Where did you get that done? Or, where did you buy that?

- You really know a lot about this area. I'm curious, what motivated you to learn so much about this?

129

How do you know if your compliment was well received, or if you stuck your foot in your mouth? A good compliment will elicit:

1. A quick smile in return.

2. A "Thank you!" or other kind comment.

3. An extended discussion about the compliment you gave, or they give you back a compliment as well.

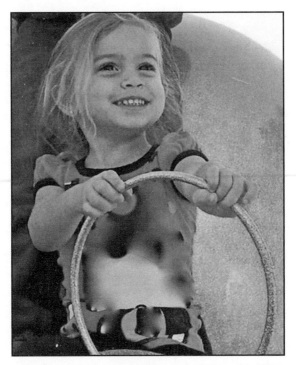

You think my shirt is cute? Thank you, I picked it out myself!

After you compliment someone, watch and listen carefully for their response. If they receive it well, they will communicate to you that you are a good listener, and that you understand them. If they hesitate or pause, or disagree with your statement, they may be telling you that you don't really understand them. A good compliment will elicit a genuine smile from most people. If you get no smile at all, that is a signal that your compliment may not have been that good. There are always exceptions to this rule, though it is rare that someone is that good at hiding their emotions. Most people will plainly show how they feel about things.

Did you get a real or a fake smile after your compliment? The easy way to tell you are getting a real smile in return is that it feels good! As we discussed, a genuine smile will incorporate the eyes, while a fake smile usually will not include tightening of the eye muscles. Laughter is also a good sign, and weak laughter is a sign you may not be communicating well. If you make someone have a belly laugh that is genuine, that is a good indication that you are building great rapport!

Is it Working?

Your gut will tell you immediately how you feel after engaging with someone. If you work hard to build rapport with someone, and listen to what they say, you will know if this is someone who you get along with. Here are a few basic questions:

1. Do you feel uplifted and inspired or drained and tense after talking to this person?

2. Did you have a lot of "Yes's" or "No's" in the conversation?

3. Does this person smile a lot, a little, or not at all?

Building rapport is much easier to do with people who smile a lot. That doesn't mean it isn't worthwhile to build rapport with those that don't smile much. Non-smilers can be great friends, you just have to dig a little deeper to find out what it is they actually do allow themselves to smile about. It can be fun to go on a treasure hunting expedition to find out where their hidden rules of happiness may be!

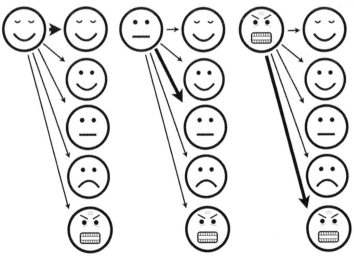

We tend to gravitate to people that behave and act like we do. Are your facial expressions building or breaking rapport with those that you want to spend time with?

Just as important as building rapport is not breaking rapport. What areas do you tend to break rapport with other people? Be honest. All of us break rapport, usually more often than we think. Be aware that breaking rapport can actually build rapport if you discover and address the situation promptly and appropriately. Sometimes we break rapport with ourselves and fight with our inner voices. For example, we want to eat something delicious, yet we are overweight and this upsets us. A part of us wants to eat, and a part of us wants to fast. This causes us to break rapport with ourselves, and it makes us feel bad (and takes away our smile). Or, we are in a relationship that doesn't serve us. We keep going back for comfort or convenience because the relationship feels good or meets a need. A part of us wants to leave, and a part of us wants to stay. It does not feel good to be conflicted and out of rapport with ourselves. Perhaps our body is out of shape and hurting, and we need to restore our body with exercise and a healthy diet. Yet, we are so busy at work or the office, we feel we don't have time to invest in our greatest asset, our physical body. These conflicts will drain our energy until we reconcile them. When our behavior matches the needs we perceive, we feel much better because our actions are in rapport with our thoughts and feelings. And when we feel better, we smile more. :)

So how did it feel to explore more deeply into your environment and those people you spend the most time with? You will quickly understand who are the people that will give to or take away from your smile. Once you surround yourself with a supportive environment and peer group, the next step is to be present yet again, this time with your "Why!" My kids are like a broken record, when I tell them to do something and they say, "Why???" So now it is your turn to ask that question, because when you know the why in your life that brings out your smile and makes your heart race, you won't have to worry about motivating yourself. Your drive will be replaced as you are powerfully drawn to what you seek in life. So let's put on our detective hat, turn the page, and start asking our "why" questions to bring out our smiles. :)

DOCTOR'S ORDERS:

1. Find a supportive environment to bring out your best smile.

2. Send positive energy to others and their response will tell you their mindset and how frequently (or infrequently) they smile.

3. Use your smile as a powerful tool in building rapport.

4. Rapport comes from getting people to say "Me Too!" or "Yes!" or by making them smile!

5. Practice giving compliments to build your relationships, and it will tell you a lot about the people you choose to spend time with.

SMILE REFLECTIONS:

• Is your environment supporting or detracting from your smile?

• In what areas can you improve your rapport building skills?

• Can you remember the last time you played or acted like a child?

I have a LOT of reasons why to smile!

chapter five

Be Present with Your "Why" to Create More Smiles

"What magic there is to smile into the eyes of a loved one! Have you done this lately?" — Dr. Rich

"The only normal people are the one's you don't know very well."
— Alfred Adler

Do you know your "Why" for smiling?

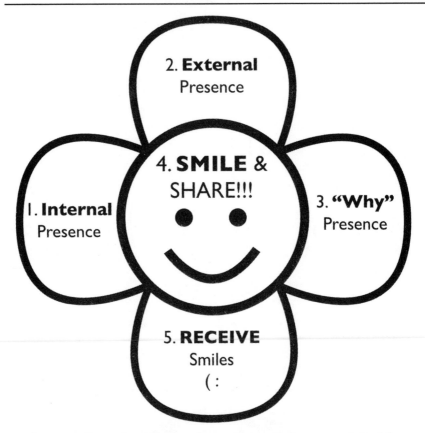

The Smile Blossom: Five Easy Steps to Making Anyone's Smile Bloom

Step 1: Be present internally. Develop the presence of your "Smile Bud." Listen to and focus on understanding your body and yourself.

Step 2: Be present externally. Unfold your petals, expand your presence and focus, and be open to your environment and those people around you.

Step 3: Be present with your "Why." Pollinate your world with empowering meaning.

Step 4: SMILE and have fun with it! Enjoy your flowering beauty and create a bouquet of smiles by helping friends and family to smile with you.

Step 5: Receive and complete the cycle of happiness with a "Thank You." Validate and encourage others to grow their smile blossoms, smile bouquets, and happiness.

Now that you know how to be present with what is external to you, have you decided to add or remove any locations you visit, or peer groups you spend time with? We always have options, and usually more than we think! Mastering the first two steps, being present with yourself and with your environment, are key. The next step in building your smile foundation is to define the reasons "Why" you should be smiling! When you take the time to ask the right questions, kind of like "Smile Forensics," you will learn what consistently makes you (and those around you) smile or frown. So let's get to work, we have some repeat frown-offenders we need to track down!

What in your life, in your future, or in your past is worth smiling for? Some people know the answer, and some don't really think about it. Even if you know the answer to what makes you smile, do you focus on it, or do you ignore it? When we focus on our reasons to smile, it doesn't seem like work to use our smile muscles. Let's take our "Why" investigation a little further. Gloria's story is a great example of how our "Why" can make us smile anytime in any circumstance.

Gloria's Smile

When we made the exciting decision to expand our office, I needed to sign some documents for the new equipment and office space. The bank sent in a representative to help get through the mountain of paperwork. In walks Gloria with a huge smile on her face, a folder of documents, pen in hand, ready to go! In seconds you could see that she was passionate about what she does. All of the legal terms and conditions of these deals can be so intimidating, but Gloria knew the document drill very well. Gloria made me feel much more comfortable with the whole process, and it all started with her genuine smile. :)

I was curious so I asked her, "Gloria, you have such a beautiful smile. Do you mind if I ask why you seem so happy all the time?" Her answer surprised me. "Well, thank you, Dr. Rich. I am happy most of the time. But it hasn't always been this way."

"I was in a miserable relationship for many years and I literally forgot how to smile. Can you believe it? One day someone asked me 'Who are you mad at?' I didn't respond. Although later I finally realized I was resentful and mad at the world for my situation in life. It didn't hit me until my granddaughter, Emily, asked why I didn't smile, and my daughter Lily responded to her, 'Grandma is just waiting to go to heaven.' I was so hurt by that comment, I spoke to my daughter after Emily went to bed. We had a heart to heart, and I finally realized that because I never smiled, everyone thought of me as unhappy, and they were right! Well, I decided I didn't want to feel or look like that anymore, and finally realized being happy is a choice I get to make every day! I smile because I choose to, and the alternative is not acceptable to me. My life is far from perfect, but I have a lot to be thankful for, and that is what I choose to focus on."

Gloria certainly does make that choice to be happy as she is smiling every time I see her. She is so energetic. She was recently planning on taking a road trip across the country, and to hear her describe it made you want to jump in her RV and join the fun! Gloria has made her smiling and happiness a lifetime choice. When Gloria was unhappy, she never felt she had a reason "why" to smile. When she realized this, and how much she loved her family and wanted them to be happy, she found her important "why" she needed to smile. She wanted to be a role model and a source of happiness that inspires her family, and not bring them down. Have you been thinking about your reasons why you should be smiling more?

"I'm always like this, and my family was wondering if you could prescribe a mild depressant."

Why Smile?

Reasons for smiling exist in everyone's life. We choose either to acknowledge or ignore them. What circumstances or relationships do you have in your life that makes you smile? Do you take the time to acknowledge the things in life that you are thankful for? Are you grateful for the loved ones you spend time with, and do you show it to them? Do you have abundance in your life, whether it be health, financial, time, relationships, or whatever else you value?

Our relationships, friends, and family can be a great source of smiling in our lives. :)

You can always find the positive or negative in any situation. Are you channeling positive or negative when you create your empowering meanings? We can focus on the smallest upsets in life to the point that it dominates our consciousness, and that makes us frown. Unfortunately this is quite common even though we live in a society with so much abundance. It doesn't take wealth, education, or social status to put a smile on our face, or even share a smile. If you look around it isn't hard to see people that have a lot of wealth, education, and social status that still don't smile that much. What's up with that? Sad, isn't it? When it is so simple to get up in the morning and put a smile on your face, why would we settle for anything less? That is one thing we are in total charge of! We don't have to pay for it, we don't have to get permission to grin, it is all you! So what are we waiting for, let's be present with our reasons "why" we have to smile and indulge in a smile right now!

In many areas of our world, people go out of their way to hold the door open and insist you go through the door first. That always puts a smile on my face! Doesn't that make you feel good when someone goes out of their way for you? But, unfortunately, there is the other side of human behavior in our world, where people are taking lives and committing atrocities. Regardless of the bad things happening out there, we

139

must press on and make the most of what we have to smile about! There will always be reasons to smile or not smile. Where we choose to focus and take action is all about our perspective, and focusing more on positivity and smiling will gives us the advantage to overcome our challenges.

Sometimes the reason "why to smile" we choose is as silly as taking a spontaneous selfie. (: This is my favorite way to tell my kids they need to wipe their mouth :)

When people ask me why I am smiling, here are the reasons that I give:

1. I love my family.

2. I am grateful for the many gifts and people and resources in my life.

3. I am thankful for my body and my health.

4. I am appreciative to live in a free country.

5. I am thankful there is something silly or funny about this situation. (there is always something to laugh about!)

Let's make up your *happy list!* It's fun and it makes you aware of what you're grateful for.

Here is the good news and the bad news. The good news is that genuine smiling shows:

1. Happiness

2. We Care About Someone

3. Confidence

4. Self-Control

5. Faith

6. Forgiveness

7. Charisma

8. Truthfulness

9. Self-Respect and Pride

Bottom line, it is our job to smile and invite others to smile too! The bad news is that sometimes we choose not to express these feelings and traits! Smiling is a full time job, and it does take some work and effort. But it also pays more dividends than any other job you can ever imagine. :) Last years smiles are paying today's dividends!

I have found that there is only one habit for *happiness*...and that habit is smiling! Think about it. Anything that you do that makes you happy involves a smile. If you like a sport, reading, a relationship, your work, or your family; they make you smile, right? Here's an example for you to say with a smile on your face: "I love my life, I have a wonderful family, and I have so much to smile about. I am both grateful and HAPPY!"

Now, imagine reading that sentence again without smiling. Not quite the same, is it? When we look at a picture of people who are all smiling, we often say "they look so happy!" And why do we tend to think kids look so happy? Because they smile so much. Act like a kid and you will feel like one, which means you have to smile just as much as they do. :) Kids run and frolic, they daydream a lot, and they play make-believe much more easily than adults because they don't think deeply and analytically like adults do. If you want to smile like a child, you must behave and act like a child. :)

One of the greatest challenges to smiling is that people are compulsive thinkers. We think about everything and tag a meaning onto every event or detail we observe. Happiness at its core does not require thinking, but it does require smiling.

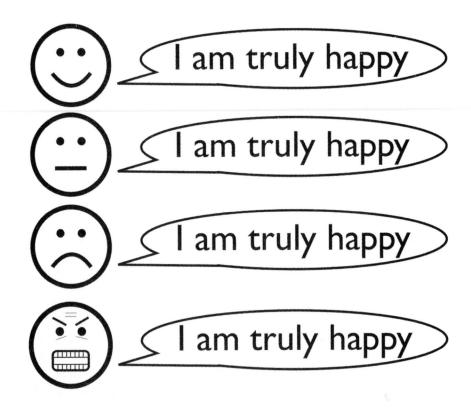

Consider how your facial expression impacts how you feel and communicate. Does your facial expression bring you up or down? If you want to be happy, make sure your facial expression agrees with how you want to feel.

Smiling and Showing that We Care

"People don't care how much you know until they know how much you care." — *Theodore Roosevelt*

How can other people know that you care about what you are doing, or that you care about them? A smile is certainly helpful if you want to demonstrate that serving or giving makes you happy. I recently ordered food at a very busy restaurant, and there was a long line out the door. The staff looked a bit frenzied and shell shocked. They were moving fast and did not take time for niceties. Unfortunately none of the servers were smiling. I got to the front of the line and they asked me plain-faced, "What can I get you?" It felt like they were saying, "Let's hurry this up, there are ten people behind you so move-it or lose-it!"

When you see people working and they look strained, stressed, or miserable, it is hard to feel they really care about what they are doing. They may have really cared about the food preparation and the overall quality, but it did not show. This is important in many areas of our life. If you love someone, a family member or close friend, and you never say it or show it, do they feel loved by you? Probably not. It is easy to fool yourself on this one. If you feel a certain way towards someone and you don't show it, they will not feel it. If something is important to you, and you never take action about it or even talk about it, is it really that important? What if you feel gratitude and appreciation for something or someone that is in your life, and you never say it or show it. Are you really grateful? If we love, feel grateful, or value something, and we never say it or show it, it is perceived as if we do not really care.

Performing the behaviors or rituals of love, gratitude, and valuing others will make them feel you care, and on some level it will also make you feel good as well, which of course lights up our smile! When the feeling isn't there, we ALWAYS have the power to create it. And this will only happen when we make the choice to do so. When we do not choose, we do not create, and we do not receive. I would follow up by saying:

1. Loving people do not just have love, they create it.

2. Grateful people do not just have gratitude, they create it.

3. Happy people do not just have happiness, they create it (with smiles).

4. Those who are wealthy in their relationships do not just have great relationships, they create them.

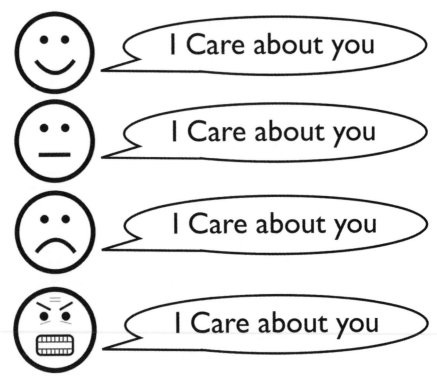

Does your facial expression show how much you really care?

Your smile has atomic power!

Smiling and Confidence

We communicate happiness through our body language like jumping for joy or falling down laughing—and it all starts with a smile. Few things show confidence more than a solid smile. When you speak of something you feel strongly about, the ability to add a smile to your face allows you to show you are self-assured and in control. On the other hand, the lack of a smile communicates that you may not feel confident in the situation. Your body language either tells others that you are comfortably in control or that you have some subtle reservations or concerns about what is going on. The stronger your smile, the better you communicate your confidence.

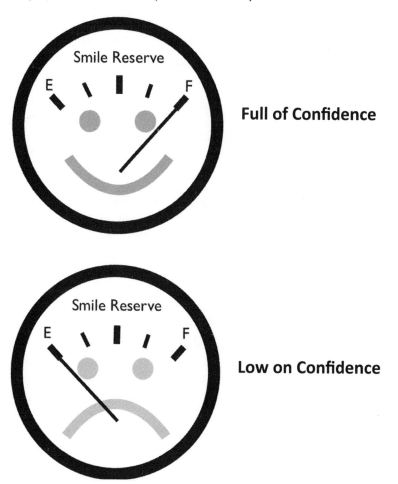

Full of Confidence

Low on Confidence

Is Your Confidence and Smile Gas Tank Full or Empty?

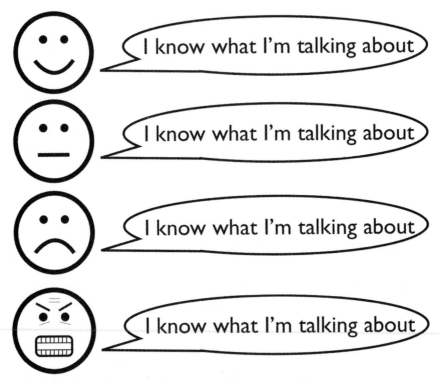

Which face inspires the most confidence in you? Which face would you rather work with or have on your team? The same words said wearing a different face have an entirely different meaning.

Smiling and Self-Control

The greater your ability to genuinely smile at a moment's notice, the greater your self-control. Smiling absolutely shows self control. There are many times that it is not easy to smile. When you feel ill, depressed, stressed out or confused, smiling may be the last thing on your mind. Some people don't have the wherewithal to smile when they're feeling down. When you show that you can smile anytime you need to, you will always be the one who everyone else looks to for inspiration and confidence.

Smiling doesn't just show self-control, it helps build it. It's a great way to interrupt your self-destructive patterns. When you are angry, sad, stressed out, or overwhelmed, as I've said many times before, one of the easiest ways to break out of these patterns is to fill your Smile Prescription. It is worth repeating: **The best time for us to smile is when we want to smile the least.**

I love teaching my kids about smiling and self-control and I discipline my kids with smiling. My two boys are normal kids, and they fight with each other like I did with my brother. Our job as parents is to step in and teach them how to work through their frustrations. Here is a common scenario:

"Okay you guys, go to your room, and when you are back in control, you can come downstairs!"

They start crying, faces scowling, stomping their feet and yelling, "I'm in control, I'm in control!" trying to avoid going to their room.

I reply, "You're in control? Okay, if you are in control, then show me your smile..."

At this point, it is very interesting to see that they are physically unable to put a smile on their face. They can't smile at all because they are not in control. As parents we get a lot of practice in breaking up fights between our kids, so I have posed this melt-down smile challenge quite a few times for them. I've challenged them so often that now they actually try to smile, even though they're angry, have tears on their face, and are scowling. They do their best to muster up-turned lips, and it ends up crumpling their whole face. It's so funny, it usually breaks their melt-down pattern and they actually start laughing themselves, getting one step closer to being back in control. Interestingly,

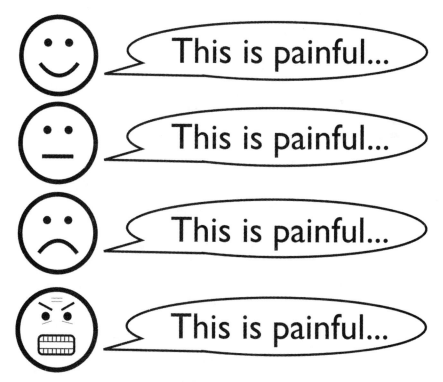

Have you ever put a smile on your face when it is difficult to do so? It takes a lot of strength and self-control to smile when we feel physical or emotional pain. Sometimes we are strong for ourselves, and sometimes we are strong for others.

many (if not most) people walk around not fully in control of themselves. Certainly they control where they walk or where they go. But are they in control of how they feel?

We mentioned in chapter one how people often walk around like they are in captivity, playing the victim and they are definitely not in control of themselves. Looking at the zoo animals can seem sad if they appear unhappy living in captivity. People-watching unfortunately can make us feel the same way about human beings, locked in the cages of their mental patterns, feelings of hopelessness, and lack of smiling.

Here are some of the most common areas where we may start to feel or act on autopilot without much strength or self-control:

1. Driving in stressful, heavy traffic.

2. Arguing with others.

3. Getting upset with ourselves for mistakes we keep repeating.

4. Eating too much comfort food

Whatever experiences you have where you feel a bit stressed, tired, or out of control, start smiling and identify that you may not be acting in your own best interests. Sometimes just a brief pause is enough to redirect us to behaviors that are more in line with our identity and better support us. Like having a quick nap, meditating, taking a shower, or exercising—smiling is a great way to improve your self-control by interrupting your self-destructive patterns and taking you off autopilot. :) Self-control is a great reason "why" many of us want to and need to smile more.

Claim your smile and break through the bars of emotional captivity!

Smiling and Forgiveness

Forgiveness is the gift we give ourselves. My kids and I love the song from the classic Disney movie *Frozen* that I believe is about forgiveness. Every time I hear my niece singing, "Let it go, let it go…" it puts a smile on my face. Everyone really needs to "let it go," especially if you want to forgive. The greater your smile is, the more easily you will be able to forgive. You can not hold a grudge and a genuine smile at the same time. Forgiveness is a physical act. The presence of a smile where there was once pain signifies that forgiveness is real.

I really understood the meaning of forgiveness when a close loved-one passed away and he named me in his will. He was a wonderful man who was very generous and I loved him dearly. And, as if the pain of his loss wasn't enough, there was a dispute regarding the will and the estate. You hear about people fighting over estate matters, and now I was about to follow the same messy and embarrassing fate. It made me sick to think we might have to go to court over it. Every time I thought about it I was tense, and my stomach churned. I refused to let money or material things control me, yet why was I so upset by it? The matter got even more complicated when hurtful things were said by those involved, words that you never want to hear when you are burying a loved one. I wasn't smiling very much during this time, though I needed to. There was hurt on all sides, and it was just messy. I made a decision that changed my life forever. I decided to forgive, let it all go and then everything worked itself out. If I had held on, we would have wasted money fighting and made ourselves sick with anger in the process. When you forgive, you can forget and your smile will come back naturally. Forgiveness absolutely is the gift that keeps on giving.

Even though you stepped on my toe, I still forgive you!!!

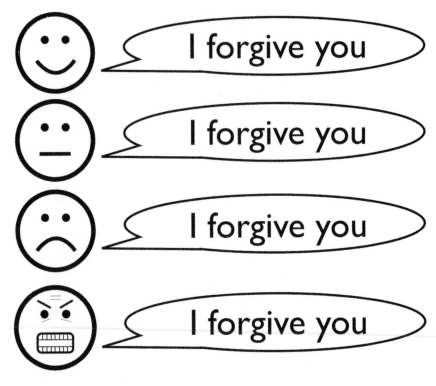

Which face do you feel looks forgiving?
Who looks like they have really let their hurt go?

When you think of someone that you feel has wronged you, what mask do you wear? The mask of resentment or the face of forgiveness? Sometimes we feel we have made mistakes that are unforgivable. Have you forgiven yourself for mistakes you made in the past? When do you think would be a good time to do that? How about now? Forgiveness is the gift you give yourself. You know you have successfully forgiven someone if you can genuinely smile around that person. Let's hear it for-smiling, and let's start for-giving. Doctor's orders! :)

"When you can smile on the mistakes of the past, whether from yourself or from others, you have forgiven. Dr. Rich

Which one is more believable to you? The face of forgiveness, or the mask of resentment?
You must smile to truly forgive.
Forgiveness is the gift we give ourselves.

Smiling and Faith

Smiling absolutely shows faith. Faith is one of the most powerful forces in human nature, and it has driven people to do things that are both wonderful and tragic. Whatever your faith is, research has shown it is healthier to believe than to disbelieve.[1] When we absolutely believe and feel strong in our faith, the certainty and security makes us smile. Face up to the sky, eyes closed, hands open, palms up, and a smile on our face is a universal sign of a believer. **The greater your smile, the greater your feeling and display of your faith.** And if we lose our faith, it will wipe the smile right off of our face. When you believe, the most powerful physical manifestation of this is that you allow your smile to show your faith for you. Your smile says what words would never be able to say. No matter what you believe, Faith plays a role in the lives of the majority of people in our world.

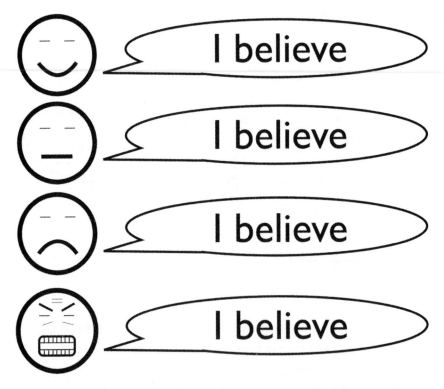

Faith is belief in the unseen. When we truly believe, it makes us smile.

Smiling and Charisma

Smiling + Energy + Rapport = Charisma. Charisma is the compelling power that some people have that attracts and excites us. We are attracted by smiling faces. So if you aspire to increase your charisma or influence with those around you, then your best bet is to put a smile on your face. We do not feel compelled to follow someone that does not excite us. And we will not follow someone that does not make us feel good.

Smiling and Sincerity

Smiling shows sincerity and truthfulness. How can smiling show truthfulness? Consider how children communicate. With few exceptions, if a child is happy and smiling, they are generally telling the truth. It takes more mental effort to tell a lie, and if they have to work that hard, it usually wipes the smile off of their face. Adults are the same way. We get an uneasy feeling about a person if we think they are lying. It takes more effort to lie, and most people are not good at it. There are always circumstances where we will be fooled, but those that do choose to lie to our faces

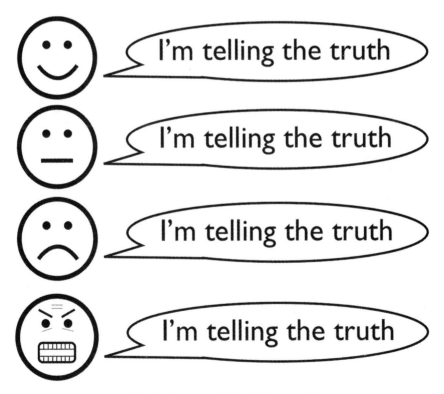

Who looks more believable to you?

are often discovered and may never be trusted again. It goes without saying that we should strive to tell the truth in all that we do, and when you communicate with a smile, it tells others that what you are saying is truthful.

Smiling and Self-Respect

It is important to treat yourself well and feel good about what you are doing. Too many people today lack respect for themselves, and will allow anyone to do anything to or for them. If you don't feel good about yourself and give yourself the respect you deserve, will you feel proud about what you are doing and accomplishing? Probably not. This is why smiling is so powerful. It sends an important message to our brain:

"Hey, I feel good about myself!"

"I am proud of who I am and what I am doing!"

"I am important and have value, and I am not settling for anger, frustration, or overwhelming emotions."

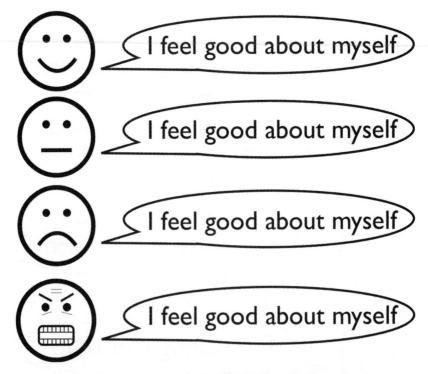

To look in the mirror and know that "I feel good about myself," is a very powerful state of mind. If we want others to feel good about us, we must create that inside of us first. Which face do you wear when judging your self-worth?

154

Smiling is in Your Job Description

Another important reason why to smile is that it's everyone's job to make other people smile. Whatever you do in life, raising your family, serving, teaching, or creating, how do you know if you did a good job? A great benchmark is you know you added value if those you are serving smile at what you do. If they like your work they will smile, refer business to you, and return for more. If they aren't happy, they won't smile, they won't send their friends, and your business or job opportunities will shrink.

At Work, We Are All Salespeople

We are ALL in sales whether we know it or not. The question is, "How good of a sales person are you?" And what is your job as a salesperson? To make your boss, customer, client, or patron smile! Sales is the transfer of emotion. What emotion do you want to transfer in your business? If you want your business to grow, you better make sure your clients are smiling. First impressions certainly count more when smiling. So what are you selling? Are you selling it with a flat face, or with a smile?

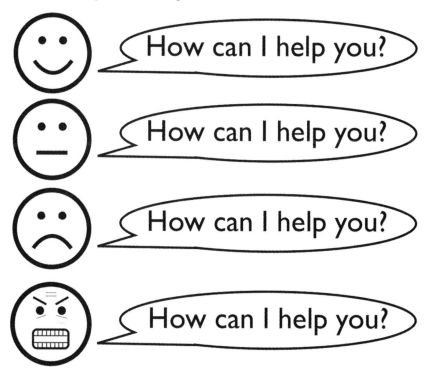

Customer service does not exist without a smile. Any job you hold or business you own is about customer service. If you do not make your customers, bosses, or coworkers consistently smile, you're not doing your job!

155

Have you found your "why" reasons to smile? Just to recap, here are the reasons we should smile more:

1. Happiness

2. We Care About Someone

3. Confidence

4. Self-Control

5. Faith

6. Forgiveness

7. Charisma

8. Truthfulness

9. Self-Respect and Pride

Bottom line, it is our job to smile and to invite others to smile too! You are now graduating to the fourth step of the smile plan in the *The Smile Prescription* and that is to actually *SMILE!* It makes me feel like school is letting out for the summer :) We have learned to be present with ourselves, our environment, and our "Why." Now it is time to have fun putting it all together. Last and final warning: once you start smiling more, you will never be the same again :) See you in the next chapter!

DOCTOR'S ORDERS:

1. Everyone has great reasons to smile! Make sure you focus on these reasons and do not ignore them.

2. Do you use your smile to show confidence, self-control, faith, forgiveness, charisma or happiness to those who matter most in your life?

3. Look around for people that look like they are living in captivity. Can you make them smile?

4. Create the strongest reasons you can for smiling. The stronger your reasons, the more you will smile.

SMILE REFLECTIONS:

• What are the things you are most confident about in life?

• Can you forgive people who made mistakes in the past?

• Do you have areas in your life that you have not forgiven yourself for?

• What is something that you believe very deeply and brings a smile to your face?

chapter six

YOUR SUPERHERO SMILE

"Reasons for smiling exist in everyone's life. We either choose to focus on them or to ignore them." — Dr. Rich

"The words you speak become the house you live in." — Hafiz

Your face, not your words, is your best storyteller. What story are you telling?

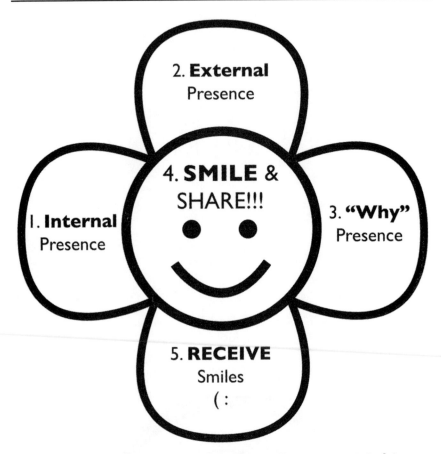

The Smile Blossom: Five Easy Steps to Making Anyone's Smile Bloom

Step 1: Be present internally. Develop the presence of your "Smile Bud." Listen to and focus on understanding your body and yourself.

Step 2: Be present externally. Unfold your petals, expand your presence and focus, and be open to your environment and those people around you.

Step 3: Be present with your "Why." Pollinate your world with empowering meaning.

Step 4: SMILE and have fun with it! Enjoy your flowering beauty and create a bouquet of smiles by helping friends and family to smile with you.

Step 5: Receive and complete the cycle of happiness with a "Thank You." Validate and encourage others to grow their smile blossoms, smile bouquets, and happiness.

Okay, you know what to do here, and yes, it is just that simple. Everyone can benefit from *The Smile Prescription*, and as we know from *Annie,* "We're never fully dressed without a smile." Now, have you ever tried to write your name or brush your teeth with your non-dominant hand? It will feel a bit uncomfortable at first, but with practice you will feel natural and get quite good as you change your routine. The same is true with smiling more frequently than you normally would. It will feel funny or strange at first, but don't worry. :) When it comes from the heart, the idea that you want to make other people smile more will make you appear more genuine and caring than ever before!

Whether you are starting your morning looking in the mirror, walking down the street, checking e-mail, eating, or getting started at work; find a way to fit more of your smile into your routines. And what do you do when someone asks, "What are you smiling for?" You can tell them about the abundance in your life. Tell them you are trying to get them to smile. Or, you can have fun and keep them guessing, "Wouldn't you like to know?" You don't have to be overbearing with your smile. The easiest way to engage people is with the micro-smile—just enough of a smile to show you are happy, but not over the top. When some returns a smile to you, that is an easy invitation to brighten your smile even more and acknowledge the smile in others.

It just breaks my heart because it seems like so many places in today's world are in the "dark ages of smiling!" Many people just don't smile as much as they could. And your smile can light up a room or brighten someone's day. The funny thing is, most people don't realize what you are doing, and they just smile along with you! Once you experience the power of smiling, you will never want to go back to the ordinary life of an expressionless face.

So, can you feel your smile muscles getting stronger? We have learned so much about being present internally and externally, why we need to smile, and how to channel the best of our inner voice. So let's get our smile on, and I thank you for your enthusiasm if you have been smiling ahead of schedule. :) There are always some students looking for extra credit!

Sweet treats can help us tune into our smile!

Tune Your Smile

You know how some musicians have a great ear and can tell you what notes are being played and if they are in tune? That ability always blows me away! When this skill is practiced and perfected, one is considered to have "perfect pitch." We may think we have a pretty good ear, but when we start singing in the car or in the shower, our family and friends remind us that we do not have perfect pitch. It still feels good to sing in the bathroom or in the car, even if we are off key, so don't stop those solo performances, rockstar!

The way our brain recognizes and identifies music is very similar to our ability to recognize and identify emotions and feelings in others. Some people are really good at reading the emotions of others, and some are tone-deaf when it comes to deciphering what people are feeling. If you rehearse your smile just as much as someone that hones their ear and develops perfect pitch, you will vastly enhance your ability to read the emotions of others, and of yourself. But life is not a dress rehearsal, so let's put on a show to remember!

Practicing your smile makes you much more aware and tuned in to where the happiness or humor is in what life throws at us on a daily basis. Some people can find smiling or comedy in virtually anything. It absolutely comes with practice. Now let me ask you a question; compare the people you know who smile with people who don't smile much at all. Who would you rather spend more time with? Are you ready now to hone your inner "perfect smile?" No one wants to be tone-deaf when it comes to smiling and happiness. Let's do this!

Where to Smile More? Proud or Embarrassed

When I get up in the morning I walk into the bathroom and I look in the mirror. With my tired face and sleepy eyes, I flash my best morning smile, point my fingers at my reflection and say "Heeeyyyyy!!! Who is that guyyyyyyy?!" My wife puts her hand on her forehead and just shakes her head. That is my cue to start a little dance in front of the mirror for my at-home audience to see. It's always a big hit, and I love being the star of my own show! At least it makes my wife smile! And it makes me smile, so I don't care what other people think! I am proud of my smile, even if I embarrass myself (and sometimes my family) in the process. :) So whether you feel proud, embarrassed, or both, you are on the right track. Keep on smiling, and the more you do, the better you will feel. You simply can't overdose when it comes to bringing out your genuine smile!

Start In The Mirror

When you look in the mirror, what a great opportunity to practice your smile! Try it, it feels good. Can you make yourself laugh? It is definitely very silly to smile in the mirror. It is a minor detail that it is socially unacceptable to be foolish and entertaining when you are all by yourself. Some people think this is weird and abnormal, but many of these same people also think it is normal to walk around all day mostly wearing a flat or expressionless face. Which group do you want to belong to?

I hear them now as they stand outside the door, "Are you talking to yourself in there? What is going on?" Don't worry, if someone questions you when you practice, just bring them in on the fun. Smiles are guaranteed when you practice smiling in a mirror with a family member or a friend. :) And I promise you, no one will be sent to the funny farm for over-smiling. At least I haven't been committed yet...

**Silliness is one of the most direct pathways to smiling (:
Have you put on your clown nose lately?**

163

Your smile has universal appeal!
Share your smile across the Solar System (:

Pets Make Us Smile

Another easy way to bring out your smile is with your pets! Isn't it amazing how animals can make us smile? I love to tell the story of a special kind of pet that brings out our smile. Susan is a patient of mine that raises and trains dogs that help the blind. Susan is in her sixties, smiles a lot, and is every bit as friendly as the dogs she trains. Her dogs are so amazing, they know that when they are wearing their vest, they are working and that they can't run around sniffing everyone they see. These seeing-eye dogs help the blind walk in stores, cross streets, and get around town. Susan said that wherever she goes with one of her guide dogs, she is always the center of attention. She then shared the following story with me:

"One day, I was training Bailey at the mall, and this woman came up to us and asked, 'Hey, I'm curious, why is your dog wearing a vest?' I turned to her with a big smile on my face and thanked her for asking. I told her that Bailey is in training to be a guide dog and is almost ready to go to work. We got to talking, and the woman told me she has a friend who is blind, and she wanted to help her adopt a guide-dog. We made plans for all of us to meet the next day.

"When we got together I introduced Bailey to Jennifer, the blind woman, and he immediately took to her as if they had known each other forever. I asked Jennifer if she would like to take Bailey for a walk and she was delighted. I gave her Bailey's leash and he guided Jennifer down the mall. About fifty feet away they turned around, and I could see that Jennifer was crying. As they returned, she said, 'Oh my gosh. This is amazing! You don't know how much this means to me. I can't wait to take Bailey home.' Jennifer reached down with a huge smile on her face and hugged Bailey. Right then I could swear Bailey had a huge smile on his face too as he wagged his tail. Bailey seemed right at home; all of the training he received had certainly paid off."

Pets Make Us SMILE!!

Not only can animals help the blind, but they also have an impact on the global stage. Consider the G-20 summit in Australia, where we saw world leaders meeting about tense situations and world crises. You don't typically see a lot of smiling and laughing at these talks. Yet, they did a photo shoot with the world leaders holding Koala bears, and not only was it super-cuddly on an international scale, but - WOW - what a lot of beaming smiles these animals brought to the most powerful leaders in the world! Even Vladimir Putin got in on the fun, and he was one of the biggest smilers in the group!

Let's face it, animals are great icebreakers. And so are smiles. If you are ever uncertain about the path you are taking in life, your smile is the greatest guide-dog you will ever have, and it will always lead you in the right direction. Unfortunately, too many people are emotionally blind, and they have no idea what they are missing.

Other Ways We Can Bring out Our Smile

When you engage in conversation, give yourself the opportunity to share a pleasant smile with this person. It tells them:

1. I care about you.

2. I care about what you are saying.

3. I want you to be happy like I am happy.

You will strengthen that relationship immeasurably, and you don't have to say anything creative to do so. Just smile! :) And you can absolutely hear a smile when someone talks. If you are on the phone, give that person a smile they will not forget! If you are in sales, you have heard the famous line, "Smile and Dial!" Well here is a little reminder for when you make that next call:

Smile and Dial! You can absolutely hear a smile in your voice!

Smiling at the Office

When you are interacting with colleagues or making a presentation, are you ever so serious that there is no room on your face for a smile? We have all been there. You can give yourself the gift of delivering that presentation with the quiet confidence that you know what you are doing. What says this better than a pleasant smile? You know you are delivering value, you know how to do this better than the competitors, but are you communicating this effectively to your team, your clients, and your boss?

Selfie Smile

Ever wonder why the selfie revolution is so big? The camera technology certainly helps. People like selfies because they make us smile and feel good! A selfie is just another reason to smile for ourselves and for those we care about! People have normal faces on, yet when someone puts a camera/phone within arm's length, the faces automatically squeeze together, and out come the smiles, especially when there is more than one person in the picture!

We were at our kids' basketball game with good friends of ours and their son, Abe, who also plays on the team. Before the game, we were talking, and I spontaneously took a selfie with little Abe. When we saw our faces on the screen, we both had a good laugh, and I coaxed him even more, "Wow, look at that SMILE! Come on, let me see your TEETH!" Then he smiled even bigger and I took another selfie and sent it to his dad who got a big kick out of it.

Selfies are more intimate, and when you can see your face that close to the camera it is guaranteed to make you smile even bigger. Smiling almost to the point of laughter makes it a more memorable photo! Have you seen a selfie with flat boring faces? Not too common, is it? So let's practice our selfies! I do my best to take selfies in the office with my team or with patients to lighten the mood and raise spirits. Works like a charm!

The earlier we start smiling in our relationships, the better!

Smiling for Your Relationships

So do you have a relationship that could use more smiling? If we are being honest, all of us have at least one, if not a dozen, relationships that can benefit from a little more happiness. And what is the first step? You engage that person with your smile! If the smile doesn't come back, what do you do then? The secret ingredient to make someone smile is to be aware that it is all about them and has absolutely nothing to do with you! Do you know what makes them smile? What makes them laugh? Where do they spend their time? What is it they love to do? If you find the correct answers to these questions, you can make them smile. :)

Our relationships make us SMILE!

Customer Service Smiles

When we get (and give) good customer service, it makes us smile! Customer service does not exist without a smile. One of the ways to get your best customer service is BYOCS - Bring Your Own Customer Service. We go to restaurants and stores and expect good customer service, right? If the store doesn't provide good customer service, they will go out of business! Yet, all of us have experienced bad customer service at some point in time.

If you always bring your BYOCS with you, it can help take the stress out of dealing with those that are challenged in the smile department. Of course we can always go to another business, but let's face it - once we have been standing in line for 15 minutes, we are already pretty committed. Sometimes we just have to make the best with what we have. And does it really help when someone messes up your order or provides bad service to aggressively voice your displeasure and give them a hard time? I believe we can do this in a more elegant and positive way. :)

You never know what may be going on in that person's life. Financial stresses, physical challenges, family matters, etc. can all build up and affect their attitude. What a gift you can give them by being kind and showing your customer service smile. Sometimes that is all it takes to turn a day around for someone and give their smile a jump-start. If we have an attitude of gratitude, then we have a lot to give. So let's start giving!

ED FISCHER

Recycle your smile, and use it over and over again. (:

Smile Variety

Now that we have gone through a variety of smile scenarios, it is helpful to talk about the diversity of smiles that are out there! Here are a few different types of smiles that are helpful to know. Just like the Eskimos have dozens of words they use to describe different varieties of snow, we also have subtle yet important distinctions we make for different types of smiles. Here are few of the basic smile types just to get you started:

1. **Micro Smile** - Almost like the *Mona Lisa* smile. Usually closed lips, with just a hint of a smile. This is a good smile for entering a room of non-smilers. A micro-smile helps you to maintain rapport. You can wait until you get a smile response before cranking up your smile to the next level.

2. **Regular Smile** - This is a broader smile that clearly shows your grin. This is the most you can smile without showing your teeth.

3. **Teeth Smile** - Yes, this is when you show your…teeth!

4. **Jaw-Drop or Open Mouth Smile** - just as it says, you smile and drop your jaw at the same time. Often accompanied by raised eyebrows.

5. **Dancing Smile** - Your smile gets better when you are waving your hands, moving your legs, and putting your body in motion! Words cannot describe it, you just have to get to work in front of the mirror and you will see what it is all about. You know what to do. :)

6. **Laughter** (hard if not impossible to do without a smile)

   g. Giggle (heehee)

   h. Chuckle (haha)

   i. Chortle (hoho)

   j. Guffaw (HAAAAAA, HAAAAAA, HAAAAAA, HAAAAAA!!)

   k. Hernia laugh - you literally need stitches, please consult your doctor.

7. **Spaced-Out Smile or Blank-Stare Smile** - this is for advanced practitioners, and it is just like it sounds. Stare blankly off into the distance with a glassy-eyed look, and put a simple smile on your face. People will definitely think something is wrong with you, but when you do this correctly, it will make you feel so peaceful, content, and happy.

So let's use this smile progression as listed above - the smallest micro-smile requires only a little bit of stimulation, and the other smiles require more energy. In general, the bigger your smile, the better you feel! So let's stimulate those faces and activate our smiles!

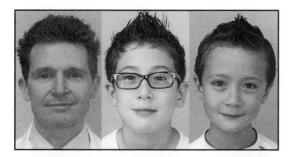

The Micro Smile helps you to keep smiling while maintaining rapport with those around you.

Regular Smile

Teeth Smile

Open-Mouth or Jaw-Drop Smile

Reasons Not To Smile - (Are You Kidding Me?!?)

Objection Management

It absolutely amazes me when I ask someone during a facial consultation to show me their beautiful smile and they flat out refuse! It's unbelievable how many different reasons people have for not smiling! Sometimes people need more than one invitation. That is okay, I have a lot of invitations to give. And I absolutely love getting smiles from the objectors. :)

Often these smile objections come from our inner voice/critic/bully, even if we do not understand why we feel this way. Many times we inherit these voices from our past, or because someone said something or did something harsh to us. It can stay with us as a deep-seated memory that subtly pesters us and brings us down. It's worth mentioning again how our greatest bully often lives inside of our head. All too often our inner bully can be very sharp, and find fault, disapproval, or pessimism in the situation at hand. It's almost as if our inner voice has verbal diarrhea, blurting out inappropriate or negative comments at the most inopportune times. It is only when you are really present with yourself that you'll be able to hear your inner bully, even when he or she is only whispering to you. The bottom line is that you need to trust your smile and don't give in to your fears. It is harder to be afraid when you are smiling, so don't let your fears control you! If you hear a smile objection, as long as you aren't hurting anyone's feelings, the correct response is to smile through it, plain and simple.

Are you forcing me to smile?!?

We aren't forcing you to smile, we are *inviting you* to smile!

OK, if you are INVITING me to smile, here it is!

Sometimes a simple invitation is all we need. (:

172

Acting Becomes Real

"All the world's a stage, and all the men and women merely players." — As You Like It, Shakespeare

As you are living your life, you represent yourself as someone who practices acting happy, acting sad, acting angry, or all of the above. Whatever we practice with enough consistency and intensity will become a reality. The weak child that spends years in athletics or in the gym will grow strong. The child with a learning disability that loves reading and becomes a proficient reader will flourish. The person that smiles every chance they get will become a happier person.

Gratitude, abundance, thankfulness, and happiness are a choice. If you believe you cannot choose, you are right. If you act grateful, thankful, happy, and with abundance, you will reap what you sow, and it will show in the authenticity of your smile.

There are two ways to cast yourself on this stage called life. One is as an extra and the other is the star. But many people, by not smiling, choose to be an extra when it would be just as easy to smile BIG and become the star. If you stop smiling, you can develop a "debilitated smile." You must use it or lose it. That is why it's so easy to tell who the stars are in life. They are so quick to smile in both comfortable and uncomfortable situations. There is no question; we always look better when we are smiling. So let's do the best with what we've got and become the STAR in our lives. You've heard the saying, "Dance as if no one is watching" and we should also SMILE as if no one is watching. Or as if everyone is looking because you will make them smile too!

I Can't Make a Good Smile for the Camera

Can't is a stop word. It's the killer of success. Whenever you say "I can't" you're absolutely right. It keeps you from moving forward. The excuse I hear the most when someone pulls out a camera to take a picture is, "I don't know what it is, I can't force a smile." I have a cure for this: When you face the camera, just smile, and shout loudly and enthusiastically in your head (or out loud), "I don't give a DAMN what people think about me!" All you have to know is that once you smile, whether it seems fake or not, mother nature will take over. It absolutely works. Just do it!

The challenge is, when we care too much about what others think about us, we're in our head, and it literally stops the flow of our happiness and internal magic. You've heard the phrase, "Just Do It," made famous by Nike. Our equivalent is "Smile Through It." If it feels strange or bad, and you want to make it better, just smile through it. This applies universally in almost any situation in life. :)

173

How is my smile in this picture?

If Jaden Can Smile, Anyone Can

Jaden is a six year old boy from Savannah, Georgia who lost his father at age four and his mother at age six. His aunt now cares for him, and after attending his mother's funeral, Jaden got tired of seeing so many sad faces. He asked his aunt how he could make more people smile, and they created the "Smile Experiment" to see how many people they could make smile. Jaden's goal is to get 33,000 smiles, and he even asked his aunt to buy some toys to give away and help others to smile. After all he has been through, watching Jaden rise above his grief to give away toys and ask people to smile would soften even the hardest of hearts. He has received so much love and smiles in return, his aunt says it is truly amazing how this light's up Jaden's face and his heart. He is well on his way to reaching his goal and making the world a better place. Jaden is a true inspiration of the power of the Smile, let's join him lifting up this world, one smile at a time!

Whew! What a great smile workout :) Did you have fun? I sincerely thank you for joining us on this smile adventure. Just one more step to go, and this last but not least step is very important and often left out. Help us complete the "smile cycle" by paying it forward in Chapter seven. This next step will be your insurance policy to help you never return to a life of "undersmiling" or "flat-facing" in today's world. See you there!!!

Let's smile through it and make the most of what we have!

DOCTOR'S ORDERS:

1. If you hear a smile objection, there is always a way it can be turned into a smile.

2. Self-conscious smiling means you care too much about what others think of you. If you are self-conscious about your smile, give yourself the gift of not caring what others think about you!

3. Acting foolish and silly are smart things to do if you want to practice your smile!

4. The situations where you want to smile the least are when you need to smile the most.

5. There are virtually no situations where a smile will not ultimately play an important role.

SMILE REFLECTIONS:

- Do you control your anger, or does it control you?

- What are your smile rituals? (i.e. smiling in daily habits)

- Are you using a variety of smiles? (Micro, teeth, open mouth, body/dancing)

- Are you practicing and sharing your smile every chance you get?

chapter seven

SMILE
HARVEST

Receive and Reap Your Rewards

"We enjoy spending time with those who share their smile and make us smile." — Dr. Rich

"If you hear a voice within you say "you cannot paint," then by all means paint, and that voice will be silenced." — Vincent van Gogh

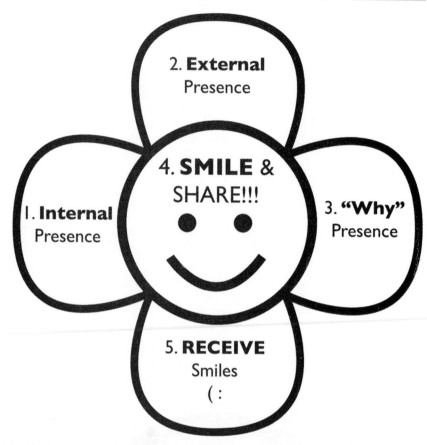

The Smile Blossom: Five Easy Steps to Making Anyone's Smile Bloom

Step 1: Be present internally. Develop the presence of your "Smile Bud." Listen to and focus on understanding your body and yourself.

Step 2: Be present externally. Unfold your petals, expand your presence and focus, and be open to your environment and those people around you.

Step 3: Be present with your "Why." Pollinate your world with empowering meaning.

Step 4: SMILE and have fun with it! Enjoy your flowering beauty and create a bouquet of smiles by helping friends and family to smile with you.

Step 5: **Receive and complete the cycle of happiness with a "Thank You." Validate and encourage others to grow their smile blossoms, smile bouquets, and happiness.**

"When you give, expect nothing in return. Just the act of giving is a gift to yourself." — Dr. Rich

Cycle of Happiness

Hello my smile warriors! By now, you have discovered and practiced many tools to help you change your life and the lives of those around you. Yet there is more! In this chapter, we will wrap up our five-step Smile Process with our last step of Receiving, and this last step is an important one. Including the receiving part of our Smile Process will give you powerful reinforcement that, of course, will make you smile. The biggest challenge with this step is that people either think they know how to receive, or they think it isn't important. Whatever your state of mind is, there is one simple way to make sure you are receiving, and that is by saying, "Thank you!"

Thank you for letting me play in the water!

Saying Thank You!

It doesn't take much time, it is easy to do, it means a lot to people, and it is so often overlooked. Just to be clear, how often should we say thanks when you receive smiling from someone else? The answer depends on your outcome. If your outcome is to connect more deeply with people than you ever have before, then you should say "thank you" every chance you get, all the time. But do I have to say the words, "thank you," all the time? Here are the simplest ways you can thank someone for giving you a smile, showing kindness, or doing anything for you:

1. Pause for a moment, make eye contact, and give them a smile as if to say thank you.

2. Repeat step one, and punctuate your smile with a verbal, "Thank you!" or "Thank you for sharing your smile with me!" You can also add, "You have a great smile!" This last comment usually invites a bigger smile by all parties involved. :)

3. If you want to take it a step further, you can ask them a smile gratitude question. "Thank you for sharing your smile! I'm curious, you are such a great smiler, where do you get your smile from?" If the conversation stalls, you can help them, "Some people say they get it from their family, and some because they have been through difficulties and realize how good they have it. What would you say it is for you?" Getting them talking about your "thank you" will make it more memorable.

4. If you really want to make an impact and knock their socks off, send a handwritten thank you card. If it can include a picture that is meaningful to them, even better!

These are four simple rules anyone can follow to say thank you for sharing your smile. It seems like common sense, but we don't really do this that much in today's world. Life can be tough, but your smile is tougher, and showing your gratitude for the impact others have on you will strengthen your smile foundation. We want to build your smile as much as possible so you are ready to weather the storms that life can throw our way.

I know you understand how important this is, and that you already feel changes in your life that will have a deep and lasting impact on everything you do. Now it is your turn to take the reins. I am going to let you experience the receiving of this "smile energy" as you complete the exercises below. Remember, this isn't just a book to read, it's a Smile Prescription for you to take and master. :) I can assure you that if you apply what you learn, the value is priceless. The exercises you see below are very powerful and will cause you to smile more on a daily basis so you can get the results you desire from your goals, ambitions, and relationships. I recommend you do them all, and you will be amazed at the results you'll receive. Remember, you only get out of it what you put into it. I thank you for your attention and for your commitment to being a part of the Smile Revolution! I look forward to meeting you in the near future, and please share your smile story with us (Doctor's orders!). :)

Before *The Smile Prescription*   **After** *The Smile Prescription*

Smile Exercises

Mind
Your
Mind

Do you mind what is going on in your mind? *The Smile Prescription* Questions
will help you to be more present with your thoughts.

HELLO :)

Can we work together now?

Download the full

Smile Prescription Workbook now!

www.TheSmilePrescription.com/workbook

Sign up now to receive additional content to give your smile the edge in today's competitive world. Special exercises and limited offers are available. Be the first to get the latest Smile Prescription offers and announcements! We look forward to being in touch!

The Smile Prescription Exercises includes material for each chapter. The chapter one exercises are included here as a bonus, but don't miss out on the FREE content for all of the chapters!!!

The Smile Prescription - The "Why?" Test - Chapter One Exercises:

One of the most important questions we will ever ask ourselves is "Why?" What is your Why? The energy inside of you that has brought you to read this far is truly profound. I would like to personally thank you for following your heart, expanding your mind, and sharing your smile. I am very proud of you, and I look forward to being a part of your personal growth and life fulfillment.

To satisfy this curiosity and energy that drives you, we need to ask the "Why" question. Why did you pick up this book? Why are you interested in learning more about smiling? What are you looking for in your life that made you feel that this book may help you or a loved one? Take a few minutes to write down all your reasons why.

If you tell me why you picked up this book, I will tell you why I put these pretzels in my mouth :)

1. Why did you pick up *The Smile Prescription*? Be specific about exactly what prompted you to buy the book and learn more. You must dig deeper than saying the cover caught your eye. :)

_____

_____

_____

_____

_____

_____

_____

_____

2. How would you rate your happiness on a scale of 1 to 10, if one were miserable and ten is euphoric giddy/ecstatic/happy? Why?

_____

_____

_____

_____

_____

_____

_____

_____

3. What would it take to double your happiness, and why?

    _____

    _____

    _____

    _____

    _____

    _____

    _____

    _____

    _____

    _____

    _____

4. To live the life of your dreams, how happy do you need to be on a scale of 1 to10, if one were miserable and ten is euphoric giddy/ecstatic/happy? Why?

    _____

    _____

    _____

    _____

    _____

    _____

    _____

    _____

    _____

    _____

    _____

    _____

5. Who are the people you want to see smile the most, and why?

_____

_____

_____

_____

_____

_____

_____

_____

_____

_____

6. What would your life be like if you were unable to make these people smile?

_____

_____

_____

_____

_____

_____

_____

_____

_____

_____

7. Who are the people that want to see you smile the most, and why?

_____

_____

_____

_____

_____

_____

_____

_____

_____

_____

_____

8. How will it make them feel if they are unable to make you smile?

_____

_____

_____

_____

_____

_____

_____

_____

_____

_____

_____

9. What have you tried to improve your happiness? Did it work for you? Why did this work or not work?

_____

_____

_____

_____

_____

_____

_____

_____

_____

_____

_____

_____

_____

_____

_____

_____

Very good! Now you are closer to knowing your "Why." I promise that you will receive more insight on each of these questions as you begin your journey through life using the lessons taught in *The Smile Prescription*. Your perspective will change considerably as you internalize the powerful truth of how smiling impacts every aspect of our lives.

Take a moment to consider EXACTLY what you said above. You wrote it out – now what would happen if you achieved everything you are looking for and found all of the answers to your questions? Would that make you happy? Will it bring a smile to your face? Continue with the exercises, and I promise you will find what you seek!

Let's make a list of what makes you smile right now. For me, it is my kids, my wife, a good joke, great food, being around people I care about, or a funny movie. What gets your smile going?

_____

_____

_____

_____

_____

_____

_____

_____

_____

What would you do to make yourself and other people smile as you take on The Smile Challenge?

_____

_____

_____

_____

_____

_____

_____

_____

What smile reminders do you have in your life? We have gotten a lot of mileage from our smile pillows - the possibilities are endless :)

Download the rest of the FREE

Smile Prescription Exercises at:

www.TheSmilePrescription.com/workbook

Wow! You have made it to the end of *The Smile Prescription*. And yet, this is just the beginning. *The Smile Prescription* is a life course that never stops giving. Thank you for your commitment to improving this world one smile at a time! Visit us at TheSmilePrescription.com to learn about events, products, and how to be a part of our growing Smile Community! I look forward to meeting and sharing a smile with you soon!

Dr. Rich

The Smile Dr.

Smile Prescriptions:

You can cut these out, make photocopies, and pass them on to your friends. Invite them to fill their smile prescriptions, sometimes someone may need a discreet reminder.

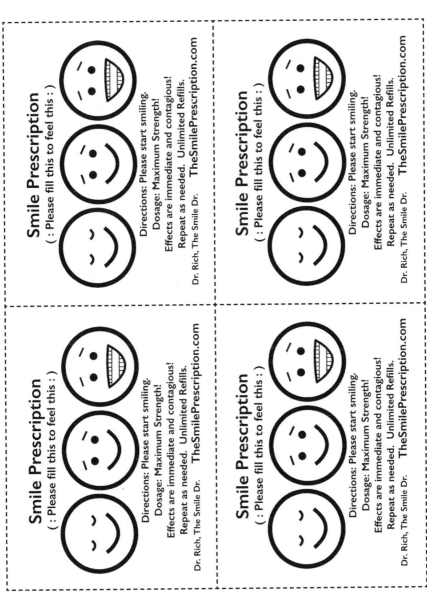

GLOSSARY

Adrenaline - The chemical that makes our heart rate go up.

Blank-Stare Smile (See Spaced-Out Smile) - Look into the distance with glassy eyes and an unfocused gaze. Now put a big smile on your face. This is the picture of pure bliss and joy!

Brainless Browsing - Escaping stress (Quadrant 4) when we are overtired by surfing the web or drowning ourselves in email or social media. Brainless Browsing drains us and saps our energy.

BYOCS; Bring Your Own Customer Service - If you get bad customer service, that is okay. Just bring your own! Add your own smile and kindness, and help someone out who is not having a great day!

Closed Mouth Smile - Smiling without showing your teeth. If you are self-conscious of your teeth, you can still put a smile on your face.

Depression - Your brain is focused more on negative self-thoughts and less on action.

Fake Smile - Smiling with the mouth and not the eyes. An insincere smile usually comes from people who care too much about what others think about them.

Flat Face - No facial expression at all. This is the expression of choice for many people walking around in their daily activities. Some people look like they are living in captivity.

Golden Rules - Do unto others as you would have them do unto you; Do not hurt other people; Obey the Law.

Inner Bully - The voice in our head that says mean things to us that we would *never* say to other people. We often think it is okay to speak harshly to ourselves, because we can say anything we want to ourselves.

Inner Toddler - A state of mind where we get upset too easily, usually because we are overtired or stuck in quadrant 4 without realizing it.

Jaw Drop Smile (a.k.a. Open Mouth Smile) - Smiling while you raise your eyebrows and open your mouth. We do this when we are really excited, like if we won the lottery, our team wins the Super Bowl, or seeing a boat come our way when we are stranded on an island.

Joy - The feeling we get when we smile.

Love - A strong desire and commitment to make another person smile.

Micro Smile or Mini Smile - Just a hint of a smile, barely there at the corner of the mouth.

Mirror Play - Practicing your smiles and facial expressions in the mirror. No better way to see what our face does!

Nose Wrinkle Smile - A playful smile.

Quadrant 1 - We are in this state when we feel peaceful, serene, and blissful; where we are smiling and our heart rate is low.

Quadrant 2 - We are in this state when we are joyful, ecstatic, and enthusiastic, and we are smiling with a high heart rate.

Quadrant 3 - We are in this state when we are sad, depressed, and down, we display a frown and have a low heart rate.

Quadrant 4 - We are in this state when we are anxious, worried, or stressed, and our frown is accompanied by a high heart rate.

Scowl - Adrenaline face. Encourages anger, discourages smiling.

Self-Conscious Smile - Someone who cares too much about what others think about them to smile fully.

Smile Transaction - You give a smile, and receive a genuine smile in return.

Smile Hunger - A practical definition for many forms of depression. When we are depressed, we are hungering and starving for a smile. When we smile, our depression inevitably improves.

Smile Reserve - How much reserve you have to smile. Someone with a high smile reserve will smile when uncomfortable or in pain. If we have a low smile reserve, we will not smile even in simple situations.

Smile Storm - A group of people all smiling and laughing.

The Smile Prescription Challenge - Make a dozen people smile, and smile in situations where you would not normally do so.

Spaced-Out Smile (See Blank-Stare Smile) - Look into the distance with glassy eyes and an unfocused gaze. Now put a big smile on your face. This is the picture of pure bliss and joy!

Is this making sense to everyone?!?

THE SMILE PRESCRIPTION GREATEST HITS

Chapter One

Beauty is that which makes us smile. We may experience something that is beautiful to our senses, or we may give a beautiful meaning to a person, event, or object. The more beauty we see, feel, hear, and touch, the more we are inspired to smile.

The healthiest of all human emotions come from smiling and laughing.

People just need to feel good. They need relief from their pain. They want comfort from their worries, tension, and stress in their life. Smiling has the ability to make us feel good. Smiling releases our tension, and smiling releases the tension of those around us.

The best way to make someone smile is to smile at them yourself!

When we change our facial expressions from stress and tension to smiling and happy, it opens new possibilities.

The Smile Challenge and your Smile Buddy will give you the keys to release the creative mind from the captivity of our culture.

More Smiling = More Personal = Longer Lasting Relationships

Less Smiling = Less Personal = Relationships Do Not Last

I like to think about depression as a *smile hunger* where our body and soul are starving for a smile. When we feed that hunger with smiles, our depression inevitably improves.

People often look like they are *living in captivity.*

As a visual society, people treat us differently based on how young or how old they think we are. We are also treated differently based on how much or how little we smile. The most important person that treats us differently based on our smiling is *ourselves.* I call this "smil-ism" or "face-ism" and you can not deny that it exists, though you can use it to your advantage.

How and why you smile shows how you live your life. When you see, hear, or feel what makes someone smile, you learn a lot about their strengths, weaknesses, and what they really are looking for.

Chapter Two

Smile for no reason and inspire wonder for those who pass by…

Proactive, genuine smiling will increase happiness, the quality of relationships, health, longevity, and emotional resilience.

Did you know your smile muscles are the STRONGEST muscles in your entire body? Even if you are able to break the world record deadlift and lift over 1,155 pounds, this will never compare with how your smile muscles can lift thousands or millions or even billions of people!

Your Face = Your Feelings.

And smiling is the most natural Botox you can get because when we activate our smile muscles, it automatically relaxes our frown muscles and forehead muscles.

You can control your feelings by controlling how you move your face and flex your facial muscles.

The best time for us to smile is when we want to smile the least.

Life is tough. Your Smile is Tougher.

Anything that takes our smile away has some degree of pain. Choosing to smile will lessen our pain and make us feel better.

When we don't care what other people think about us, it is really difficult to make a fake or strained smile.

The facts are that we have the power to change and control the meaning we give to our actions with our smile.

Mother Theresa was not considered to be a runway model, but when she smiled, the whole world smiled with her.

There is nothing good or bad, but smiling or frowning makes it so.

Some people will smile no matter what happens to them. Some people will not smile, no matter what happens to them. The difference between these two types of people is the meaning (thinking) and the *smiling* they give to their lives.

We should never let anyone or anything take our smile away.

One of the definitions of a "fake smile" is when we care too much about what other people think about us.

Do you surround yourself with things that make you smile?

Smiling is the most attractive thing we do to our face, as it literally *attracts* other people to us. Smiling also brings us compliments, and it makes us *feel good about ourselves!* So why not smile more?

The ability to smile at anything in life creates wealth beyond measure.

Twenty smiles a day keeps the plastic surgeon *and the doctor* away.

Chapter Three

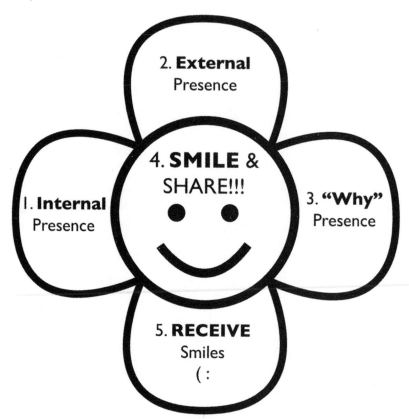

The Smile Blossom: Five Easy Steps to Making Anyone's Smile Bloom

Step 1: Be present internally. Develop the presence of your "Smile Bud." Listen to and focus on understanding your body and yourself.

Step 2: Be present externally. Unfold your petals, expand your presence and focus, and be open to your environment and those people around you.

Step 3: Be present with your "Why." Pollinate your world with empowering meaning.

Step 4: SMILE and have fun with it! Enjoy your flowering beauty and create a bouquet of smiles by helping friends and family to smile with you.

Step 5: Receive and complete the cycle of happiness with a "Thank You." Validate and encourage others to grow their smile blossoms, smile bouquets, and happiness.

Being present is the most control we will ever have over our lives. Presence is necessary for a genuine smile (:

There is great power in communicating without words (:

We often focus on distractions and ignore all the ingredients to a happy life right in front of us. Being present with our distractions is never as fulfilling as being present with what is most important to us.

Adults think more deeply and smile less. Children think more superficially and smile more.

I cannot think of a greater art-form available to humankind beyond sculpting and shaping our brain and our consciousness.

Think about the masterpieces we all create as we build and grow our character and personalities. The artistry, graffiti, noise, and quiet of our mind becomes our personality and our identity.

Sculpting and reshaping our consciousness is the highest form of human artistry. The greatest tools to prepare the canvas of our mind are presence, meditation, and prayer.

Are you clearing the canvas of your mind with your presence, or are you letting the distractions in life clutter your masterpiece?

A life without faith is a life full of doubt. No one ever lived their best life doubting everything. What do you believe in?

When you know how to be present, you can literally take a vacation anytime you want. Nothing is more peaceful and serene than what the present moment has to offer us. Presence is the greatest present we can ever give or receive.

Quadrant 1 happens when we feel peaceful, serene, and blissful; where we are smiling and our heart rate is low.

Quadrant 2 is someone who is joyful, ecstatic, and enthusiastic, and they are smiling with a high heart rate.

Quadrant 3 reveals that when we are sad, depressed, and down, we display a frown and have a low heart rate.

Quadrant 4 happens when we are anxious, worried, or stressed, and our frown is accompanied by a high heart rate.

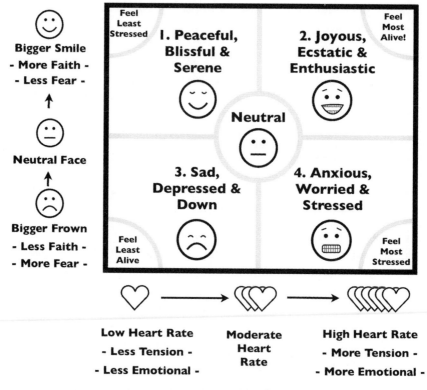

Emotional IQ & Emotional Presence - 4 Quadrants

The higher my heart rate goes, the more emotional I will feel, just as lowering my heart rate will lessen my emotional intensity.

When your body tells you something, you should listen to it!

In our world, many people are oblivious to their emotions. Take the time to be emotionally present with yourself to see and feel who you are and where you are with your smile and your heart rate.

I see this all too often in my office where people say the most awful things about themselves. We tell ourselves things we would *never* say to another person, and we rationalize that it is okay to disrespect ourselves because these words come from ourselves. Well, they don't come from ourselves, they come from words someone else said to us many years ago, and I call this voice our "inner bully."

You can not allow the bully to tell you who you are and what you can or cannot do. More importantly, we cannot allow the bully to tell us how to feel.

Chapter Four

Happiness, trust, friendship, love… You can tell all of these things and so much more about a person from their smile.

So are you the one influencing your peers' smile, or are they influencing your smile?

Clutter = Stress = No Smile

You can easily tell who the frequent smilers are in the same manner you learn how good someone is at throwing a frisbee. If you want to know how good someone is at playing frisbee, just throw a frisbee at them! If they catch it and throw it right back to you, they are usually pretty good. If they hesitate a little, perhaps fumble the frisbee a bit or drop it, and then throw it back to you, they are probably an average frisbee thrower. If they let it drop at their feet and ignore it or leave it there, chances are they don't throw frisbee that much. It is very similar with people when you throw your smile at them.

When you truly know what someone wants, you hold the power to make them smile. Just as when you know what makes someone smile, you know what they truly want. Conversely, if you don't know what someone wants, it is much harder to make them smile.

When you build effective rapport, people remember you. They will remember the feeling that they like you and they will have a reason to talk to you again.

If you can pay a genuine compliment to someone about something you share in common, you will considerably elevate your status in their eyes.

Chapter Five

What magic there is to smile into the eyes of a loved one! Have you done this lately?

Reasons for smiling exist in everyone's life. We choose either to acknowledge or ignore them.

I have found that there is only one habit for *happiness*… and that habit is smiling!

One of the greatest challenges to smiling is that people are compulsive thinkers. We think about everything and tag a meaning onto every event or detail we observe. Happiness at its core does not require thinking, but it does require smiling.

The stronger your smile, the better you communicate your confidence.

The greater your ability to genuinely smile at a moment's notice, the greater your self-control.

Have you ever put a smile on your face when it is difficult to do so? It takes a lot of strength to smile when we feel physical or emotional pain. Sometimes we are strong for ourselves, and sometimes we are strong for others.

Smiling is a great way to improve your self-control by interrupting your self-destructive patterns and taking you off auto-pilot.

Forgiveness is a physical act. The greater your smile is, the more easily you will be able to forgive. You can not hold a grudge and a genuine smile at the same time. The presence of a smile where there was once pain signifies that forgiveness is real.

The greater your smile, the greater your feeling and display of your faith.

Faith is belief in the unseen. When we truly believe, it makes us smile.

To look in the mirror and know that "I feel good about myself," is a very powerful state of mind. If we want others to feel good about us, we must create that inside of us first. Which face do you wear when judging your self-worth?

Customer service does not exist without a smile. Any job you hold or business you own is about customer service. If you do not make your customers, bosses, or coworkers consistently smile, you're not doing your job!

Chapter Six

Once you experience the power of smiling, you will never want to go back to the ordinary life of an expressionless face.

Some people think practicing your smile in the mirror is weird and abnormal, but many of these same people also think it is normal to walk around all day mostly wearing a flat or expressionless face. Which group do you want to belong to?

Silliness is one of the most direct pathways to smiling (:

"Smile and Dial" when you are on the phone so others may "hear" your smile!

You never know what may be going on in that person's life. Financial stresses, physical challenges, family matters, etc. can all build up and affect their attitude. What a gift you can give them by being kind and showing your customer service smile. Sometimes that is all it takes to turn a day around for someone and give their smile a jump-start.

We aren't forcing you to smile, we are *inviting you* to smile!

Gratitude, abundance, thankfulness, and happiness are a choice. If you believe you cannot choose, you are right. If you act grateful, thankful, happy, and with abundance, you will reap what you sow, and it will show in the authenticity of your smile.

Chapter Seven

There is one simple way to make sure you are receiving, and that is by saying, "Thank you," either with your words, your smile, or both!

Additional Smile Tools

Smile Storm

When I attended a leadership group, we had about fifty people in the room, and we made it sound like it was raining indoors. Have you ever done this before? Here is the progression:

1. You start with everyone rubbing your hands together continuously, and this sounds like the rustling wind.
2. Then you slowly have everyone start snapping their fingers together, like the pitter-patter of rain drops.
3. Starting at one side of the room, you have people lightly pat on their thighs, mimicking increasing intensity of the rain.
4. The next wave gets people slapping their thighs even harder, as the rain is coming down even stronger yet.
5. Lastly, you slap your thighs and pound your feet, and the storm is on!
6. Go from 1 through 5, then back down to 4, 3, 2, and 1 again, to mimic the passing of the storm.

It was pretty cool, and I decided I wanted to make a Smile Storm. So I did it at a few of my events. We literally fell out of our chairs it was so funny. Here is the recipe:

Tell everyone that if you look at a partner and SMILE while doing this, it helps to make it easier. It helps to have a funny leader to keep the smiles going.

1. Start by gently blowing air out of your nose (2-4 times per second) while you are smiling, as if you are laughing through your nose.
2. Then bring your mouth to say the word "he" and make a breathy laugh (like a dog panting) with the same tempo, still smiling, without using your voice.
3. Then amplify with your voice to an audible "hee-hee-hee-hee."
4. Next is a "Ho-ho-ho-ho-ho-ho."

Then "ha-ha-ha-ha-ha-ha" and amplify the sound until the laughter gets out of control!

We tried this and we didn't get past step 3 before we lost control and laughed until we cried. What was so funny anyway? We may never know, but we sure did have a great laugh. And we all felt much better afterwards too!

REFERENCES

Chapter One

1. Saha, Sukanta, David Chant, Joy Welham, and John McGrath. "A Systematic Review of the Prevalence of Schizophrenia." PLoS Medicine. http://www.ncbi.nlm.nih.gov/pmc/articles/PMC1140952/.

2. Mobbs, Dean. "Humor Modulates the Mesolimbic Reward Centers." Neuron, Vol. 40, 1041–1048. December 4, 2003. http://findlab.stanford.edu/Publications/Humor_neuron.pdf.

3. Miller, Michael, and William Fry. "The Effect of Mirthful Laughter on the Human Cardiovascular System." Medical Hypotheses. Accessed August 16, 2015. http://www.ncbi.nlm.nih.gov/pmc/articles/PMC2814549/.

4. Buchowski, MS, KM Majchrzak, K. Blomquist, KY Chen, DW Byrne, and JA Bachorowski. "Energy Expenditure of Genuine Laughter." National Center for Biotechnology Information http://www.ncbi.nlm.nih.gov/ pubmed/16652129.

5. Bains, GS, LS Berk, N. Daher, E. Schwab, J. Petrofsky, and P. Deshpande. "The Effect of Humor on Short-term Memory in Older Adults: A New Component for Whole-person Wellness." National Center for Biotechnology Information. http://www.ncbi.nlm.nih.gov/pubmed/24682001.

6. "Suicide: Fact Sheet No. 398." World Health Organization. September 1, 2014. http://www.who.int/mediacentre/ factsheets/fs398/en/.

7. Leibman, PhD, Martin. "Suicide Prevention Awareness Saves Lives." The Official Homepage of the United States Army. http://www.army.mil/article/134477/Suicide_prevention_awareness_saves_lives/.

8. "Suicide: Consequences." Centers for Disease Control and Prevention. June 10, 2015. http://www.cdc.gov/ violenceprevention/suicide/consequences.html.

9. Marcus, Marina. "Depression: A Global Public Health Concern." Paper for the World Federation of Mental Health. http://www.who.int/mental_health/management/depression/who_paper_depression_wfmh_2012.pdf.

10. http://www.who.int/mental_health/management/depression/who_paper_depression_wfmh_2012.pdf .

11. "Average Adult Manages Seven Smiles a Day... but One Is False!" Daily Mail. March 5, 2013. http://www.dailymail.co.uk/news/article-2288833/Average-adult-manages-seven-smiles-day--false.html.

Chapter Two

1. Kraft, Tara L., and Sarah D. Pressman. "Grin and Bear It." Psychological Science. September 2012. http://pss.sagepub.com/content/23/11/1372.

2. Lewis MB, Bowler PJ. "Botulinum toxin cosmetic therapy correlates with a more positive mood." *Journal of Cosmetic Dermatology,* 2009, 8, 24–26.

3. Dimberg, Ulf, Monika Thunberg, and Kurt Elmehed. "Unconscious Facial Reactions to Emotional Facial Expressions." Psychological Science 11, no. 1 (2000): 86-89.

4. VanSwearington JM, Cohn JF, Bajaj-Luthra A. "Specific Impairment of Smiling Increases the Severity of Depressive Symptoms in Patients with Facial Neuromuscular Disorders." *Aesth.Plast.Surg.* 1999;23:416–423.

5. Harker LA, Keltner D. "Expressions of Positive Emotion in Women's College Yearbook Pictures and Their Relationship to Personality and Life Outcomes Across Adulthood." *Journal of Personality and Social Psychology*, 2001, Vol. 80, No. 1, 112-124.

6. Hertenstein MJ, Hansel CA, Butts AM, Hile SN. "Smile Intensity in Photographs Predicts Divorce Later in Life." DOI 10.1007/s11031-009-9124-6.

7. Abel E. and Kruger M. (2010) "Smile Intensity in Photographs Predicts Longevity." Psychological Science, 21, 542–544.

8. Fried, Itzhak, Charles L. Wilson, Katherine A. MacDonald, and Eric J. Behnke. "Electric current stimulates laughter." *Nature*, February 1, 1998, 650.

Chapter Three

1. Bonelli RM, Koenig HG. "Mental disorders, religion and spirituality 1990 to 2010: a systematic evidence-based review." *J Relig Health.* 2013 Jun;52(2):657-73. DOI: 10.1007/s10943-013-9691-4.

2. "Meditation Programs for Psychological Stress and Well-being: A Systematic Review and Meta-analysis." *JAMA Intern Med.* 2014;174(3):357-368. DOI:10.1001/jamainternmed.2013.13018.

3. Roemer Lizabeth, Orsillo Susan M., Salters-Pedneault Kristalyn. "Efficacy of an acceptance-based behavior therapy for generalized anxiety disorder: Evaluation in a randomized controlled trial." *Journal of Consulting and Clinical Psychology*, Vol 76(6), Dec 2008, 1083-1089. DOI: 10.1037/a0012720

4. Bowen et al. "Mindfulness Meditation and substance use in an incarcerated population." *Psychology of Addictive behaviors* 2006; 20, 343.347.

5. Tapper K, Shaw C, et al. "Exploratory randomized controlled trial of a mindfulness-based weight loss intervention for women." *Appetite* 2009; 52, 396-404.

6. Britta K. Hölzel, James Carmody, Mark Vangel, Christina Congleton, Sita M. Yerramsettia, Tim Gard, Sara W. Lazar. "Mindfulness practice leads to increases in regional brain gray matter density." Psychiatry Res. 2011; January 30; 191(1): 36–43. DOI:10.1016/j.pscychresns.2010.08.006.

7. Carmody, J., and RA Baer. "Relationships between Mindfulness Practice and Levels of Mindfulness, Medical and Psychological Symptoms and Well-being in a Mindfulness-based Stress Reduction Program." *J Behav Med.* 2008; 31, no. 1, 23-33.

8. Luders Eileen, Kurth Florian, Mayer Emeran A., Toga Arthur W., Narr Katherine L., Gaser Christian. "The unique brain anatomy of meditation practitioners: alterations in cortical gyrification." *Front. Hum. Neurosci.* 2012; 29. Feb. DOI: 10.3389/fnhum.2012.00034

9. Britta K. Hölzel, James Carmody, Mark Vangel, Christina Congleton, Sita M. Yerramsettia, Tim Gard, Sara W. Lazar. "Mindfulness practice leads to increases in regional brain gray matter density." Psychiatry Res. 2011; January 30; 191(1): 36–43. DOI:10.1016/j.pscychresns.2010.08.006. .

10. Zatorre R.J., Fields R.D., Johansen-Berg H. "Plasticity in gray and white: Neuroimaging changes in brain structure during learning." *Nature Neuroscience*, 2012; 15, 528-536.

Chapter Five

1. Brick Johnstone, et al. "Relationships Among Spirituality, Religious Practices, Personality Factors, and Health for Five Different Faith Traditions." *J Relig Health* DOI: 10.1007/s10943-012-9615-8

Other Sources

American Psychological Association. "Marriage and Divorce." http://www.apa.org/topics/divorce/.

Aparna A. Labroo a, Anirban Mukhopadhyay, Ping Dong, "Not always the best medicine: Why frequent smiling can reduce wellbeing." *Journal of Experimental Social Psychology* 53 (2014) 156–162.

Carnegie, Dale. *How to Win Friends and Influence People* New York. Pocket Books 1998.

Darwin, C. R. *The Expression of the Emotions in Man and Animals* London, John Murray, 1872.

Golda Stefan M, Zakowskib Sandra G., Valdismarsdottira Heiddis B., Bovbjerga Dana H., "Higer Beck depression scores predict delayed epinephrine recovery after acute psychological stress independent of baseline levels of stress and mood." *Biological Psychology* 2004, Nov. 67;3. 261-273. DOI:10.1016/jbiopsycho.2003.12.001

Haukka Jari, Suominen Kirsi, Partonen Timo, Lonnqvist Jouko. "Determinants and Outcomes of Serious Attempted Suicide: A Nationwide Study in Finland, 1996-2003." *American Journal of Epidemiology* 2008; 167, 10, 1155-1163.

Hebb, D. O., *The Organization of Behavior* 1949.

James, William The Principles of Psychology 1890. chap 25. http://psychclassics.yorku.ca/James/Principles/prin25.htm

Kemp Janet, Bossarte Robert. "Suicide Data Report, 2012" Dept. of Veteran Affairs Mental Health Services Suicide Prevention Program. 2012.

Lee Taekwan, Cai Lili X., Lelyveld Victor S., Hai Aviad, Jasonoff Alan. "Molecular-Level Functional Magnetic Resonance Imaging of Dopaminergic Signaling." *Science* 2014; 344; 6183. 533-535 DOI: 10.1126/science.1249380.

McIntyre, Christa K., Roozendaal, Benno. "Adrenal Stress Hormones and Enhanced Memory for Emotionally Arousing Experiences." *Neural Plasticity and Memory: From Genes to Brain Imaging* Boca Raton, CRC Press. 2007.

Morton, Brian. "Falser Words Were Never Spoken." *The New York Times*. August 29, 2011. http://www.nytimes.com/2011/08/30/opinion/falser-words-were-never-spoken.html.

Newport, Frank. "In U.S., 77% Identify as Christian." Gallup.com. http://www.gallup.com/poll/159548/identify-christian.aspx.

Rushton J. Phillipe, Bons Trudy Ann. "Mate Choice and Friendship in Twins: Evidence for Genetic Similarity." *Psychological Science* 2004. 16;7. 555-559.

Strack F, Martin L, Stepper S. "Inhibiting and Facilitating Conditions of the Human Smile: A Nonobtrusive Test of the Facial Feedback Hypothesis. *Journal of Personality and Social Psychology*, 1988; 54, 768-777.

"What Is Extreme Global Poverty?" One Day's Wages. Accessed August 17, 2015. http://www.onedayswages.org/ about/what-extreme-global-poverty.

Xie L, et al. "Sleep drives metabolite clearance from the adult brain." *Science*. 2013 Oct. 18;342, 6156. 373-377. DOI:10.1126/science.1241224.

Yamada Y, Nakazato Y, Ohga A. "The mode of action of caffeine on catecholamine release from perfused adrenal glands of cat." Br J Pharmacol. 1989; 98;2. 351-356.

MEET THE AUTHOR

Dr. Rich Castellano is The Smile Doctor, and has patients from around the world that he has helped bring out the best in their smile. Dr. Castellano is an award-winning, double board certified facial plastic surgeon, and founder of ImageLift, his minimally invasive facelift and laser rejuvenation center. He has performed over 10,000 facial cosmetic procedures, including over 3,500 facelifts using the latest minimally invasive technologies. He is an experienced facial artist and takes pride in training other physicians, allowing ImageLift to be named as an international center of excellence for long-term facial fillers. His first book, *We Guarantee We Can Make You Look Younger* is a Wall Street Journal Bestseller and has been widely acclaimed as one of the best facelift resources available today.

At the age of seven, Dr. Rich endured two-and-a-half years of life in a wheelchair and on crutches, which set him on the path to improve the lives of others, one smile at a time. It was his life's calling to pursue a career in medicine, where he realized one of the most therapeutic treatments any doctor can give their patient is...their smile. He eventually overcame his personal health issues, helped his mother deal with schizophrenia, and rose above his own bout with depression. The wisdom gained from these personal tragedies inspired Dr. Rich to write *The Smile Prescription*, and he readily admits that this philosophy saved his life, his marriage, and his business. Dr. Rich is a widely sought after speaker, and takes his smile to over fifty events per year.

When he is not in the office, Dr. Rich enjoys attending church and spending time with his best smile coaches—his family! This includes his lovely wife Irene, who is a concert violinist and super-mom to their three beautiful children, Ella, Domenic, and Xavier. Dr. Rich loves to exercise by chasing his kids around, and after the kids have crashed into bed, he enjoys playing chess and acoustic guitar.

Thom McFadden, also known as Hollywood's "Coach to the Stars," has been enriching the lives and increasing the productivity of writers, actors, entertainment industry professionals, and corporate America for over thirty years. Thom is the author of Acting for Real, the award winning book the New York Times called, "Remarkable!"